To Ann,

all the Me.
always!

Greg

GREGORY L. PSALTIS, DDS

A Personal and Professional Memoire of
"Dr. Sawdust," a Pediatric Dentist

INTO AND OUT
OF THE
MOUTHS OF BABES

Into and Out of The Mouths of Babes

© 2022 Gregory L. Psaltis, DDS

Paperback ISBN: 978-1-66783-987-5
eBook ISBN: 978-1-66783-988-2

INTO AND OUT OF THE MOUTHS OF BABES

PREFACE

My career as a pediatric dentist was an unlikely one. Had anyone suggested to me during my college days that I would spend 45 years diving into the mouths of children and loving it, I would have had serious doubts. As this book will describe, that is exactly what happened.

Every name mentioned in the narrative of this book has been altered, although I am certain that former patients and parents of my practice as well as colleagues will be able to identify themselves and celebrate their place in my mind and heart. Names appearing on letters and pictures are the real people's names, but last names have been blanked to preserve identities. Some stories may be slightly different than the exact events since I may have combined more than one situation into a single story. However, every detail included in this book actually happened. I have long professed that if a person is a pediatric dentist and has eyes, ears and memory, stories like mine simply happen of their own accord. My career enriched my life so greatly that I felt a desire to share my stories with a bigger audience than just myself. Attendees at my lectures at dental meetings will have heard some of these tales, but many of the background details will be new to most.

Dentistry is not always treated kindly by Hollywood and comedians. Root canals always score high on the worst-thing-that-can-happen-to-you list in life, and grotesque caricatures of sadistic dentists yanking teeth out of hapless peoples' mouth are common fodder. *Marathon Man, Little Shop of Horrors* and other classics do nothing to change that image. It is sad and it is unfair to a profession that does all it can to talk patients out of treatment! Nobody wants dental patients to be comfortable as much the dentists themselves.

While it is an unrealistic goal to turn the opinions of all people about dentistry with this single book, my great desire is to create a different picture of how profoundly it can change the lives of children. I have often pondered the fact that dentistry is unique in the health care field in that we are the only professionals who see people at regular intervals when they are healthy. If a child was sick, the appointment would be canceled. In this unusual and wonderful way, it ensured that the interactions between the dental team and the children began in a positive way.

As will become clear throughout this book, it is also a story about opportunities and people appearing at the exact right moment to redirect my thinking and encourage my movement forward in life. I cannot overstate how grateful I am to the many people who influenced, taught, and inspired me during my career. It is often only in retrospect that I can acknowledge these angels who appeared at the right time for me. I have always thought I was a self-directed person, but as the following pages will make clear, my self-direction was often disrupted by my own impatience or lack of a vision beyond what was right in front of me. The course corrections I experienced over the years were pivotal in reaching the place where I could assemble so many stories, many sweet and entertaining, others heart-wrenching and difficult. I am grateful for my own willingness to listen to the wisdom of others and recognize forks in the road that I hadn't even seen before. This, alone, is a lesson in life.

Because of these moments, this book is not only about dentistry per se, but is also about aspects of my life that render the book both a personal as well as professional statement. It is a memoir from a dental perspective. I always enjoyed talking with my patients and their parents about topics we held in common. They might have included living in Arizona, attending an opera in Vienna, Austria or doing crossword puzzles. I always felt that those discussions added to the connection I shared with the people who came into my practice. Those threads will appear in this book as well. I trust it will demonstrate that I am *person* as well as pediatric dentist.

Finally, I want to add that it would be inaccurate to say I loved every minute of my career. Children have vomited on my lap, bitten my fingers, screamed at a pitch only rivaled by a jet engine, and clamped their mouths shut in the fashion of a bulldog. Anyone who practices dentistry for children and claims that it has all been dreamlike is simply not telling the truth. It can be challenging, and it can be frustrating, but above all else, it has been gratifying far beyond my expectations. I am very grateful that key people at key moments pointed me toward this specialty. I hope the following stories will help the readers grasp the joy and the satisfaction I have experienced.

Greg Psaltis
Olympia, Washington
March, 2022

I dedicate this book primarily to my wife, Mary Ellen, and my children, Erica, Reid and Kosta, all of whom lived with me during my time-consuming career. I also dedicate this book to those courageous people who stepped up at the right times in my career and impelled me forward instead of letting me wallow in my depths. Finally, I warmly dedicate this book to all the children who were my patients as well as the parents who entrusted their precious offspring to my care. It has been an honor to embrace that trust with all my energy. I also want to include all the supportive team members who took this journey with me. I couldn't have done it without them.

INTRODUCTION

Muy especiál

"Muy especiál, muy especiál," her grateful father said to me over and over while vigorously and enthusiastically shaking my hand. I was afraid his enthusiasm might result in dislodging my shoulder, but I was grateful for his lively response. His wife merely sat and stared at me, sobbing and daubing the tears from her eyes. It was yet another special moment for me and perhaps the crowning one of my career. It reflected on all I had learned, experienced, and enjoyed during my career as a pediatric dentist. Just like the father's assessment of me, it was "very special" for me as well. It encapsulated so much in a brief moment. How could I ever explain this to others?

I begin toward the end of my career experiences simply because retrospection leads to introspection, taking away the busy moments of one's life when appreciation and understanding may fall away in the midst of "doing." I have filled so many teeth, reluctantly extracted many and "counted" innumerable teeth (the euphemism for an oral examination) that I revel in the memories of my career choice that brought me so many more rewards than I could have imagined. Even in my moments of self-doubt or in my moments of undue optimism, I had never dared to conceive of the satisfaction that my work ultimately brought me. Many may regard being a dentist as unthinkable. "How can you work in people's mouths?" they often ask. At least I'm on the better end of the alimentary tract in my opinion. Others would question my choice of specialty. Learning that I was a pediatric dentist, some would pose the question, "So you only see children?" Yes. Their next question would be "why?" My answer was simple, unexpected, but entirely truthful. "Because the alternative is seeing adults," I would say.

Pediatric dentistry is certainly dentistry. It involves the many aspects of oral care that one traditionally assumes would be done by a dentist. The technical details of my career were repetitive, mostly simple and, after my first few years, not all that interesting. I always took it very seriously, but the aspect of working with children that never failed to hold my interest was the interaction with the young patients. I also cherished the opportunity to *create* the attitude toward dental care rather than *change* it. Many of the parents who brought their children into the practice were unabashedly fearful while their children sat quietly and happily during our attention to their teeth. I always felt fortunate to welcome patients who still had not yet developed an opinion about dental care and guide them to a place of genuine accomplishment and confidence. In the end, it was always the best work I ever did. Many of the teeth I treated ultimately fell out, but the attitudes I nurtured were far less likely to exfoliate like baby teeth. It also thrilled me to witness parents watching their children accept care with such facility. I'm sure some parents doubted their own children's resilience and perhaps also doubted their own, with haunting memories of dental experiences in their own past. Then, before their own eyes, they could witness their three-year-old having a filling done without difficulty. Much credit was given to me although the true accomplishment should have gone to the children. After all, I had the easiest part. They were ones having the procedure.

I refer to the procedures I did in my practice as the *fundraiser* to support the really important work I was doing. There were no fees for building a child's confidence. That was merely a part of the package. Dentists get paid for what they do with their hands, but those in my specialty get paid in other-than-financial ways for what we do with our voices, our words, and our encouragement. At times it feels magical, and I have wondered exactly how it works. As a speaker on the dental continuing education circuit for more than 27 years, I have stood in front of audiences talking about techniques to instill positive attitudes in children's minds, but in the end, it really is all about one's own attitude. The cute terminology I used ("sleepy juice" for local anesthetic and "whistle" for drill) made things understandable for my young patients, but if delivered with a sense of irony, embarrassment, or lack of conviction, they would fail to achieve the desired result. It is a choice that a professional makes to either embrace the fun of caring for children or not. Dentistry tends to attract technophiles and that is not always congruent with warm and fuzzy. When the warmth and fuzziness come out in a genuine way, the results can be astonishing, if not "muy especiál."

Through a lengthy process that is described later, I began caring for children in Mexico solely for my satisfaction. My career had provided so much that I felt it would be rewarding to export my skills to populations that truly had no hope for dental care and would be both appreciative and attentive. After establishing a toehold in Zihuatanejo, Mexico, I created a project in Cabo San Lucas, which brings us back to my opening story. It has been my experience that stories tell more than just the facts, and, in pediatric dentistry, people can easily identify with such stories because they are principally about human nature, not fillings and crowns.

Early on in the Cabo San Lucas project, a child presented for examination. Her name was Magdalena and she was about 15 years old. Magdalena is a child with autism. Both Mr. and Mrs. Lopez warned me in no uncertain terms that Magdalena had never cooperated with any doctor or dentist so that they had little to no optimism about the chances for success with her visit with me. In fact, these are the cases that I like the best because there is no chance of failure! If the appointment doesn't accomplish anything, the parents are not surprised. However, any success, no matter how small, will be seen as something "very special." My team of three (myself, a dental hygienist and another dentist) greeted Magdalena as she entered the room, in part of her own accord, and in part due to the physical assistance of her father. She was a girl who we considered too big to physically overcome and I knew immediately that she would be a black or white case. In the face of resistance on her part, my two female cohorts and I would not be able to restrain her and keep her safe with the sharp and high-speed equipment we used. Once in the dental chair, Magdalena showed no signs of enthusiasm for what we proposed. My style with all children of special needs is to treat them like every other child. After all, who really knows what these children understand or not? The fact that children with autism do not communicate with us verbally has never meant that they cannot understand us.

I believe it was the tone of our voices and the gentle, slow pace of our process that helped this girl to understand at some level that we were not a threat. Once her mouth was open, I could examine the child, understanding that I was undoubtedly the first person to ever look at her teeth—often a challenge no matter the age. I was pleasantly surprised and pleased to find her in reasonably good oral health, although she did have some minimal cavities on her permanent molars that required our attention. The purpose of this first visit was only to evaluate both the dental condition as well as the emotional response. I told Mr. and Mrs. Lopez that Magdalena needed fillings and that I wanted to see her again. They expressed some surprise that she had allowed us to look into her mouth but assured us that accomplishing any actual treatment was unlikely. They specifically requested the last appointment of the day so that Magdalena's screaming wouldn't frighten any other patients awaiting their appointments.

When the appointed day arrived, we were completing care on our next-to-last child when the atmosphere of the waiting room chilled as if the dementors from Harry Potter had arrived. The air was thick with apprehension, but I knew it wasn't from the girl. As our previous patient bounced out of the treatment room with a big smile on her face, the Lopez family stared at her with both concern and surprise. We prepared the room for Magdalena and when I went out to bring her back, both parents stood, as if they would be part of the treatment team. I asked them to take their seats and then guided Magdalena into the treatment room. She got into the chair without hesitation, and we began our soft-toned chat with her. I couldn't sense any fear from her, but I knew that the test would be when the care began.

Step number one in a restorative dental visit (filling, or *restoring*, teeth) is to numb the oral tissues (gums) with a topical anesthetic so that the penetration of the needle for local anesthetic is more comfortable. When I showed Magdalena the long Q-Tip with the topical gel on it, she clenched her teeth, pursed her lips, and shook her head. There is no question that this is the action that leads many dentists to reach for a referral pad to "go to the kid's dentist." However, I *am* the kid's dentist and I'd seen this many times. This neither cows nor discourages me from proceeding. As I gently touched her lips to open them, I lightly rubbed the cotton tip and continued to encourage her to open her mouth. She did exactly that. With the topical anesthetic in place, I then moved on to the injection, carefully instructing my two team members to control Magdalena's head. A sudden jerk can result in a broken needle and in the case of a child who is thrashing, it becomes a nearly impossible task to retrieve it. She held her head still while I kept whispering my soft monologue into her ear. So far, so good.

Next came the rubber dam to isolate the teeth and keep them dry during the filling process. The girl kept looking at me and I kept looking at her, communicating in our own way, ignoring any verbal transactions for the moment. Magdalena had three small areas of decay—two on one molar and the other on a second molar. Normally in my practice I would "prep" (the public calls this "drill") all three areas of decay at once and then fill all three at once. Still not knowing with certainty that our patient would remain cooperative, I told Priscilla and Joan that I would prep one spot and fill it, prep the next spot and fill it and prep the final spot and fill it. In this way, I would not have three areas of the two teeth "opened up" without fillings in case Magdalena suddenly decided she was done for the day. After about ten or so minutes, the three areas were treated and, with things going so smoothly, we placed sealants on two other permanent teeth that were also isolated. When we took the rubber dam off, Magdalena sat up, made a noise that I have since come to recognize as her greeting, and hugged each one of us.

With treatment now complete, I took the girl's hand and led her back out to the waiting room where her anxious parents awaited the report. I'm confident that they couldn't understand why no noise had poured out of the treatment room, but the moment their daughter smiled and gave them the same noise she had given us, Mrs. Lopez burst into tears of gratitude and Mr. Lopez grabbed my hand and began pumping my arm with his continuous accolades of how special I must be. It was the moment many pediatric dentists both live for and experience. We do what people think can't be done, and, when we have success on a child with special needs, the parents' gratitude is enormous. Of course, I told the Lopezes that this is simply "what we do," but they wanted nothing to do with that simple explanation. For the first time in her 15 years, Magdalena had had a successful visit with a health care professional and the faces of her parents told me all I needed to know. Did I complete fillings for this child? Yes. Was that the most important thing for me? No. To me this was the work I was meant to do and the rewards, both tangible and otherwise, filled me. To me, the work was truly "muy especial."

Magdalena at the end of her appointment during which she got three fillings and two sealants. Her father stands next to her as I celebrate with both.

Magdalena has now been a patient in the Cabo clinic for 7-8 years as I write these words and over time *all* of her needed treatment was completed. At times it was challenging, but mostly she has been a model patient. The parents continue to extol my specialness, although by now they have seen other practitioners provide care for their daughter. It was never about me. It was always about the attitude. The volunteers who come to the clinic in Cabo are all of the same mindset and all provide the same *care*. I have always maintained that in my specialty, we treat the teeth and care for the patients—two separate activities happening simultaneously. The people who participate in the project understand and practice this concept. That is why I always refer to each of them as "muy especiál."

SECTION 1- GETTING THERE

The road less traveled because I didn't have a map

Like many aspects of life, my pathway to a career as a pediatric dentist was the result of numerous moments of insight, unexpected interactions with people I hardly knew, and the good fortune to pay attention to the signs that led me to my choice. My introduction to dentistry as a child was hardly positive and the mere fact that I ultimately came to a career that had negative memories for me was only because of critical individuals stepping up to say the right thing at the right time. Had I lived only in my narrow world (or that of my father's hopes) I would never have happened upon the rewarding work that I found looking into the mouths of children and providing care for them.

Many people can trace their pathways to their own life choices, and I have little doubt that they would find common links to people, moments, and decisions that parallel mine. I sometimes wonder if William Shakespeare had someone tell him, "Maybe you should write some of your stories down," or if Isaac Newton had someone suggest to him that he sit under an apple tree. Make no mistake. I am not equating my own history with giants of their fields like those two men, but there remains a mystery about how our lives unfold and how each of us somehow reaches that point when we figure out what we want to do with ourselves. During my childhood, the pathway seemed far more linear than it is today. One needed only go to college, get a degree, work hard, and success would follow. I'm confident that formula is more elusive in today's changing world. Guidance from elders may no longer ring true for younger people who are pursuing careers that their parents don't even understand. In that way, my story may seem strange, if not inconceivable to some. It is almost inconceivable for me.

When I was a child, I loved to read biographies. It fascinated me to know how famous people spent their childhoods, moved in the direction of their life's work, and, ultimately, made a mark that made their lives worthy of publication. I read mostly about presidents and scientists since they were the ones I most admired. I presume many of us want to make our own mark, but few of us get to do so in such a public way that fame would follow. Fame was never important to me and any hint that I might hope to gain some from this book is unfounded. I will not change who I am. I hope my good fortune in arriving at dentistry for children is worthy of being told because most of us share a common desire for the good of young people. We also identify with stories about human nature. Had I been given the opportunity to write the script for the reality that will follow in this section, I would not have had the imagination to develop a story like this. The universe takes good care of us. If we spend the time to notice that it becomes all the more astonishing. I am grateful to those who played a role in my life as well as my own good sense to recognize a good thing when it was laid in front of me. The path, however, was not as linear as I had expected.

CHAPTER 1

Put your hand down…..or not

Many parents in my practice sat in amazement as their children were being treated for dental care. Some offered their own stories about how their dental history began on a less than positive note. I could not only sympathize but identify. In spite of leaving the town in which I grew up more than sixty years ago, I still carry memories that are as vivid as some that happened last week. Most of these memories are very fond ones, but my introduction to dentistry as a child was not.

I spent most of my childhood in suburban Chicagoland in a town named Elmhurst. In retrospect, it was a wonderful place to grow up, and I still honor and appreciate my Midwest values. I still feel at home when I return. My home there, at the corner of Fairview Avenue and Vallette Street, was an easy walk to my elementary school, Lincoln School. It was also a quick bicycle ride down to Rex Field, also known as "Stinky Park" due to the aroma. The water treatment plant was there, accounting for the atmosphere. Little League games were played at Rex Field, and I spent countless hours of pick-up baseball in the days when children could still play outdoors without parents worrying. All I needed to do was find at least three other boys who wanted to play and off we went. I still recall my white T-shirts coming home with the brown stain of both the dirt of the infield on the field as well as the sweat from my face as we ran around in the sweltering Illinois summers. It prepped us well for our the "real games" we played in Little League when we wore replica uninforms of real major league teams. I spent three years on the Red Sox with our sponsor, Soukup's Hardware Store, stitched on the back.

Friends lived up and down Fairview as well as Sunnyside Avenue, the next street down. We would play cops and robbers, cowboys and Indians, and many other games through the summer. At nighttime, we would catch fire-flies. On the Fourth of July, my entire family would pack up and go to the local park for the annual fireworks show. To collect our baseball cards each year, we would go to Trainor's Spotlite, a small store, locally owned by a kind and patient man named Barney Trainor. We always called the store "Barney's" in spite of its actual name. It was the precursor to 7-11's or Circle K's. It sat on the corner of Montrose Avenue and Spring Road, one of the local "business" districts. The packs of cards cost 5 cents and when I had a quarter, I would buy only two packs at a time to avoid pay-ing the penny tax. I would buy two packs, leave the store, come back, buy two more packs, leave again and finally return for my last nickel's worth of cards: no tax paid with a maximum of cards purchased. Another favorite hangout was The Candy Bar, which was exactly what it sounded like. We'd buy candy and other assorted goodies there while Wally, the owner, would look on. Once, when I was given the task of taking a six-pack of empty Coke bottles to his store to return them, I dropped one and broke it and in the process of picking up the pieces, cut one of my fingers. Wally consoled me, gave me the full refund, even for the broken bottle, put a bandage on my cut and gave me a candy bar to salve my injuries.

York Street, which was "the" main street in town, had the real business dis-trict, which included the York Theater where I watched many movies and had my first date. The Jewel Tea food store was also there, and my dad and I would always go together to do the family shopping. I knew the layout of the store by heart and my father would send me on a mission to pick up an item and I would have it back to him within moments. I believe he delighted in it. The York State Bank was on that street as well, and I always marveled at how my father could go to the drive through window, hand them a piece of paper, and get real money in return. This was magic.

To me, it all seemed like heaven.

Elmhurst introduced me to many things in my young life. I attended the brand new junior high school there, Bryan Junior High. I was elected Vice-President of the school as a seventh grader, which probably vaulted me into the social circle of the "in group." It was exciting. We had parties at people's homes, usually in the basements, and it was, as I often call it now, the big "hand-holding" phase of my life. Contact beyond that was unimaginable unless you were George S, who (shockingly) had actually kissed a girl. Phew!

As a child I faithfully brushed my teeth every night before saying my prayers, but I had never heard of floss. My mother cooked our meals and didn't let us have too many sweets. My two brothers and I often fought over the six-ounce Cokes that my mom would occasionally buy and when the Peter Wheat bread man came to our front door, she would sometimes treat us with cupcakes. I cannot recall having regular desserts at our meals, but I never felt neglected. As with most children, I felt special and, at my immature level, invincible. One of my first hard lessons in life came in Elmhurst: my introduction to dentistry.

In 1957, my dental appointment with Dr. Eric Wainwright was straightforward. By today's standards, it must seem rather shocking, but at the time, it was as normal as pedaling my bike to one of the stores on Spring Road. My mother gave me two dimes, and off I walked to the corner of Berkeley and Vallette, where the bus picked me up for the trip to York Street. I paid my dime into the meter and knew where to get off the bus to get to Dr. Wainwright's office. I was nine years old at the time, but none of this seemed strange or beyond my abilities. Once off the bus, I crossed York Street, the busiest street in Elmhurst, walked over to the multi-level building, and took the elevator up to the third floor where I would find the dental office. I was careful to keep the second dime so I could pay for my return ride on the bus back home.

Dr. Wainwright was a one-man operation. There was no receptionist, no hygienist, and no assistant. There were also no consent forms or health histories that I recall. Gloves and masks were not mandatory in dentistry at that time. All of this is hard to imagine now, but that was dentistry in 1957. My memory of Dr. Wainright was that he was young, tall, wore glasses, and had the traditional white smock that snapped at the shoulder. His hands smelled like soap. Like most dental offices of the era, he had a straight-back chair with two black arm rests, and he worked standing up. It was only years later that "sit-down dentistry" was introduced. His "drill" was a belt-driven slow speed device unlike the air turbines that are used today. When I entered dental school at the University of California in San Francisco, this relic was still in use, which brought back less-than-kind memories for me. Today, all the hand pieces, which is what dentists call the public's "drills," are air driven and much kinder to teeth.

My instructions were very simple. Dr. Wainwright explained that he would be fixing my cavities, and, if anything hurt, I was to raise my hand. No topical anesthetic was applied, and no local anesthetic was used. The issue of pain was apparently assumed to be so minimal that no intervention was necessary. To this day I talk with dentists who feel local anesthetic is unnecessary for treatment of primary teeth. My experience taught me otherwise. Since this was a first experience for me, I had no idea of what to expect, but I quickly found out. When the grinding began on an upper tooth, it seemed as though my entire head was being vibrated and the aroma was quite unappealing. The doctor continued grinding away as my senses told me that something must be wrong. The pain was building in my tooth and head, and yet Dr. Wainwright continued as if everything was just as fine as it could be. I fought the tears that I felt coming and wondered if I could just "tough it out." As the youngest of three boys in my family of origin, I was expected to act like a man, even at the age of nine. This was an era when boys didn't cry and didn't complain. These were mantras that were firmly embedded in my brain, and, as a result, I gripped the two arm rests more and more tightly as I tried to maintain control. I almost wondered if smoke would start rising out of my mouth as the heat and friction built. Finally, recalling that Dr. Wainwright had told me to raise my hand if anything hurt, I reluctantly felt that I needed to tell him how much he was truly hurting me. Loosening my iron grip on the right arm rest, I raised my hand, thinking that this would somehow make things better.

Dr. Wainwright noticed my hand but did not stop his work. I wondered if he was "almost done," a phrase I came to appreciate more deeply when I was on the other side of the treatment, but on he went. When I finally waved my hand in desperation, his response was as clear as his instructions. He stopped for just a brief moment, looked me in the eyes, and yelled in a very loud and clear voice, **"Put your hand down."**

I did survive the ordeal, but not without some visceral memories. Years later, whenever I listened to the parents in my practice express their own fears about their experiences as children, I could relive each detail of my own first time in a dental chair. The result of this was that I would have more compassion for the parents and more incentive to make sure I could deliver the needed care to my patients without their feeling pain. Dentistry had made enormous strides over the nearly twenty years between my visit with Dr. Wainwright and my graduation from dental school. The years did not diminish my own feelings, however, and I credit my time in that chair in Elmhurst, Illinois, with much of my desire to be different. I never used the technique of "raise your hand if it hurts" in spite of the belief by many parents that giving the child some control during the appointment was a good idea. More than anything, I didn't want to even suggest that what we were about to do would be painful. I was adequately aware if a child was in distress by looking at their knitted eyebrows or clenched hands. I also never began an appointment unless I was very confident that the local anesthetic was working well. Of course, there were times when children were uncomfortable, and I made it a point to check to make sure it wasn't pain. I learned that a child in pain and a child who *doesn't like* what's happening look very similar. My job was to make sure I could differentiate between those factors. My experience helped me ascertain the difference, and, while I would occasionally put my *foot* down, I never felt the best strategy was to holler at a patient to "put your hand down."

Flexibility required that I constantly learned on the fly. I am not one of the romantics who professes that they "learned everything they know from children." It was my father who taught me how to drive, Frau Charlton who taught me much of my German, and Dr. Iseman who taught me how to prepare a tooth for a crown. However, I received some instructions on holding hands up from one of my outspoken patients, a five-year-old girl. Laura marched into my office one day, and, in a most businesslike way, handed me a piece of paper. On it were her instructions to me about her own secret code in the form of hand signals. I kept the paper because it was one lesson that I did learn from a child. Laura made things clear:

When Laura raises her 1 HanD
It means she Wants to Spit,

2 HanDs Mean Drink

Laura's plan worked perfectly. The Team and I followed her instructions. The dental assistants would suction the spit out of her mouth each time one hand went up and they would squirt some water behind the rubber dam when Laura looked as if she were signaling a touchdown. At the end of the appointment, Laura gave me a hug, a smile, and told me she was glad she had the hand signals since she wasn't able to say anything with the rubber dam over her mouth. Out of the mouths of babes and, quite honestly, her point was well taken.

CHAPTER 2

What goes around....

Much like others who have influenced my life, I have had opportunities to plant seeds in the minds of young people. Sometimes these were simply thoughts about what was possible to accomplish in a dental chair and other times they were thoughts of being a dentist. It was always gratifying to learn that someone who had spent time with me had chosen to pursue the dental profession. It was also satisfying to know that even if my impact was nothing more than giving a child the opportunity to succeed in a potentially challenging situation, it was something worthwhile for the child. Some opportunities arose in a most unexpected way, as was the case in Cabo San Lucas, Mexico on the same volunteer project where I met Magdalena. Enter Elena with her winning smile and outgoing personality and I found myself in a particularly delightful situation.

That many Greeks dream of owning and running a restaurant can hardly surprise readers. It is less known, though, that an almost equal desire runs through the culture that is not as widely understood. This dream is for the children of Greeks to become doctors. From the time I have any memories at all, I recall my father constantly telling me, "You're going to be a doctor." In many ways I have always appreciated that advice, since it unburdened me from having to pick a major in college or figure out what I wanted to do as a career. It took me years to figure out that this admonition was a double-edged sword. That enlightenment didn't come to me until I was a college student, but I digress.

Growing up near Chicago, the entire Greek side of my family got together with regularity—at Greek Easter, at Thanksgiving, at Christmas, at weddings, baptisms, birthdays, and sometimes for no reason at all other than to get together. These were unusual times. I had the good luck of having a cousin who liked me so that I had an automatic companion each time we visited. My mother, who was the only non-Greek in the entire clan, and my two older brothers, neither of whom spoke the language, would sit and listen to the lively, if not heated, conversations that rolled out among all the others, who were entirely comfortable with the language of their heritage. I can't say I was oblivious to it all, but generally I was too busy playing and awaiting the delectable meal that my Yiayia (Greek for grandmother) would be preparing.

My father had an older sister, a younger brother, and a younger sister. Both of the sisters married physicians, which also fed the idea that Greeks become doctors. Both owned nice homes in Chicago proper and one typically hosted the family get-togethers at his place. Mostly in retrospect did I fully appreciate that he was often in his own small office space in the house, sitting on a recliner, and not always in the middle of the festivities. He was born in Greece, a Spartan, and was not the life of the party. He always did have time for his patients, though, as did my other uncle. Both spoke well of their profession, and when the time approached that I needed to decide to actually pursue a career, they told me that there was "no other profession" other than medicine.

My high school days, spent in Tucson, Arizona, were enjoyable and filled with achievements. I was never like either of my brothers, both of whom were athletic. They threw the shot put and the discus, two events that never crossed my mind as I was a relatively scrawny kid. My older brother was also the football star of the team, student body president, homecoming king and pretty much everything I wasn't. I, on the other hand, ran cross country, competed in the mile run in track, and was the editor of the newspaper. None of it seemed as exciting or as "cool" as my brother, but

I enjoyed my time in high school. My activities and grade point average gained me an acceptance into Stanford University before it required multiple AP classes, straight A's, at a minimum, and the ability to play the tuba left-handed. Still, it was Stanford, and I was glad to go to the Bay Area since I'd heard so much about it.

The first thing I learned at Stanford was that nobody there was stupid. I sometimes describe my successes in high school as not necessarily rising to the top, but rather treading water and not sinking to the bottom. Harsh? Yes, but I had been trained by my father's assessments of my report cards to expect nothing less that excellence. If I brought home 5 A's and 1 B, he only commented on the B as if I had been a slacker. I found that I needed to work harder at Stanford in one week than I probably had for an entire school year at Palo Verde High School. This is not an indictment of my high school, but rather a commentary on the quality of brains at my new institution. I had always been good at memorizing things and spewing the information back on tests, assuring an excellent grade. Suddenly it felt as though I was in a different world. First year students were required to take Western Civilization, and during class discussions I had the feeling that others had read a different book than I had. I discovered that my mind was far more mechanical than interpretive. Nevertheless, I managed to perform well enough to earn a decent first-quarter GPA although it was only because I was no longer treading water, but rather swimming hard enough not to drown.

As a pre-med, I was surrounded by other earnest students wanting the same thing I thought I did—entry into medical school. I had only applied to three universities—the University of Arizona as my "ace in the hole" plus Stanford and Duke, since both had excellent medical schools. It didn't take long to wonder if I could make it into any medical school, but I continued on my path until Spring quarter. By then I had become more comfortable with my situation, but I came down with mononucleosis and spent a week or so in the Student Health Center. Naturally I wanted to get healthy again, but I also had the nagging sense of falling behind in my classes. When I was discharged, I asked some of my fellow pre-meds if I could borrow their notes from the classes I'd missed and was shocked to find out that they were unwilling. It was my first encounter with the depths of both the competition and the tactics used to get a leg up. I had long understood survival of the fittest, but never applied it to myself. It gave me a different perspective on my prospective professional peers.

During the summer between my first and second years, I took the time to research other possible careers. Since I'd never even considered any alternatives, I had no plan, although a friend, who was an attorney, invited me to shadow him one day. I wish my recovery from mono had been as rapid as my decision about law as a career. It probably only took half of that day to cement a "no way" in my mind. All of the tests I'd taken for skills had pointed me toward accounting and I know I would have been a good one since I have always personally handled books, tax forms, and other paperwork with facility. It just didn't seem to be what I wanted.

Credit where it is due. My older brother, Bill, the shot-putter and discus thrower, had long idolized Dallas Long, who was the national shot-putting hero of the United States at that time. He had competed in the Olympic Games, was the athlete of the year in Arizona, and, after his athletic career, became a dentist. Bill clearly followed in his footsteps in many ways, including choosing dentistry as a career. He had always enjoyed building models and working with his hands. He told me that he felt it was a better choice than medicine because dentists worked regular hours, didn't have to be affiliated with a hospital and had far more independence. Of course, it was convenient that the profession had virtually the identical college prerequisites. That was the germ of the idea to switch from one health-care profession to another, but the clincher came when I had returned to Chicago. While my two physician uncles had told me that I should be a doctor, their wives (my aunts) told me that if I wanted anything resembling a family life, I should avoid it. This influenced me heavily since my own experience of my two uncles was that they were often either absent or called away from family events. It was noble that they were so committed to their patients, but they did not appear to lead the same sort of family life that my father had. My dad was a tire salesman, but he was also President of our local Little League and was active in PTA and several other activities that seemed more rewarding than working late hours. The decision was made, and I announced that I had decided to pursue dentistry. This was far from popular with my father, who had clearly pinned his hopes of having a physician-son on me. It was impossible to know at the time what a remarkably wise choice that was for me, personally. While I still esteem physicians greatly, I do not envy their hours or the extent to which their practices were hampered by pressure from insurance groups.

In the end, I did become a doctor. I imagine most parents would be pleased with that, but it was obvious that my father felt I'd compromised or possibly even failed. I suppose it was much like that "B" on my report card that was otherwise filled with "A's." It just wasn't good enough, but I always hoped that he would be able to see how much I loved my work. If he did, he never told me.

History does repeat itself, though, as I discovered years later. The biggest surprise of my 45-year career as a "kids' dentist" has been how I have been filled with both joy and gratitude. If pictures can convey what words cannot, I submit here a series of photographs of a particularly engaging five-year-old girl whom I treated in Cabo San Lucas. Her name is Elena and the first picture will show the degree of fear that she (and the overwhelming majority of my patients) showed during her care.

 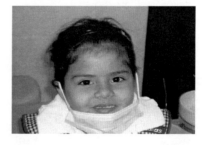

As I treated her, she continually reached up toward my face, but with the rubber dam in place it wasn't possible to understand what she was trying to convey. Each time I would tell her to put her hands on her tummy, but she continued to reach toward me. I couldn't converse with her, so I had to wait until the end of the treatment to discover that she had been trying to tell me that she wanted one of the masks that we were wearing. Of course, I gave it to her at once (second picture) and she then boldly looked at me and asked for gloves as well. The third picture shows her with gloves and a mask. With that image before my eyes, I told her that she "should be a dentist."

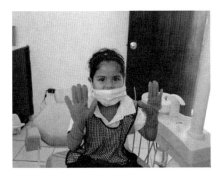 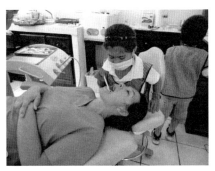

Perhaps I was channeling my father! Because my career has taught me to see things in a positive light, it might have been that fact that allowed me to believe that I saw the spark of possibility in her eyes. I imagined nobody ever mentioned that idea to her before, but even behind her mask, I could tell she had lit up. One of my fellow volunteers, Kendra, asked me what I had said to Elena because she could see the magic working, too. I told what I had said and immediately Kendra told me that she would be happy to be a "patient" for Elena, which led to the final endearing shot in this sequence. It was hard to tell who had given whom the more meaningful experience, and so it is in pediatric dentistry.

After this, it was easier to forgive my father, since I, too, had tried to spark something in a child. I don't know whatever happened to Elena, but I do know that on one day, at one time, a mutually satisfying connection was made between us that underscored the love of my work. I also knew that my father had been correct in telling me, "You are going be a doctor." While I may not have been saving lives as a physician might, I was certainly rising to my highest good in very different ways and, after all, I actually did become a doctor.

CHAPTER 3

You never know who will provide the spark

Other than my brother's recommendation and my childhood experiences, I knew almost nothing about dentistry. It seemed like a good idea, but like many good ideas, when it became a reality, things changed. Having taken my one-year "sabbatical" in Vienna, Austria, following my college graduation, I felt ready to embrace my studies again. Stanford had provided the opportunity to live in that majestic city both as a student and as a resident assistant. But Stanford had also been a humbling experience and I mistakenly felt it would be the most difficult academic work I would ever do. This proved wrong, simply wrong.

My first day in the University of California, San Francisco, School of Dentistry was an unexpected jolt when I saw that my class schedule was for forty hours per week. The mere thought that I would be in a classroom eight hours a day for five days per week was already staggering. But when it struck me that there would time for studying and, as I later found out, time to work on all the laboratory skills that the school demanded, I had some doubts. Lucky for me, I had already experienced a similar shock when I encountered the challenges of my undergraduate years. It didn't take long to make friends as I had opted to live in a dental fraternity for my first year. By doing that, it afforded me several luxuries, including breakfasts and dinners cooked each day by our tempestuous cook, Roger, and the comradery of others in the same boat. I never thought of dental school being a place of competition like my undergraduate years—after all, I had gained entrance into my conduit for a professional life. My overwhelming sense was that I had "made it" as long as I could survive.

Anatomy, tooth morphology, biochemistry, physiology, occlusion, histology, dental materials, and other heavy-weight classes made me realize that there would be no simple classes. What surprised me, though, was that so many of my classmates had already, at some level, been involved in dentistry. Some had been lab techs, some had been dental assistants, and some had served in the military, gaining knowledge and technical skills that I had hardly conceived. During my years of dental school, there was no direct patient care during the first two years. It was all academics and technical skills without ever looking into a real person's mouth. The academics were challenging from the sheer volume of courses plus the innate difficulty of each. My discipline at Stanford served me well. The techniques courses, such as how to prepare a tooth for a filling (better known to the public as "drilling on the tooth"), setting denture teeth, casting gold crowns, and giving injections, all added to the workload in a very unaccustomed way for me. It has never been lost on me that I made my choice of professions with so little understanding of what it really entailed, and it didn't take long to conclude that I may have made the biggest mistake of my life. My father's words echoed in my mind as I pondered whether or not I would be happy working in the mouths of people.

Part of the challenge was the faculty. Unrelenting in their criticism of our efforts, it felt like I imagined boot camp to be. Ironically, we were expected to do things perfectly even though we had never done it before. It was not unusual to be criticized in front of the entire class during lab sessions, battering our delicate egos and sometimes infuriating us. In moments of benevolence, I try to imagine that the philosophy was to ingrain a sense of morality in us so that we would leave the school with a strong sense of what is "right" and spend the rest of our years trying never to diverge from that gold standard. People have often told me that they have heard that the dental profession has the highest suicide rate. I never knew if that was true or not, but when you enter into a field where perfection is the standard, there isn't much room to digress without feeling guilt. There were some very kind and supportive instructors and then there were the ones that still bring back vivid memories. In a class where we learned to carve life-size teeth out of wax, one instructor would look at your work and proceed to improve it by carving on it with his pinkie fingernail. This he did without speaking but you could hear the words traipsing across his mind and they were never good. Another instructor literally told me one day that he could eat a piece of wax and defecate a better tooth than I had carved. These were not uplifting times. Finally, one of our instructors, Dr. Martin Stock, was a retired military dentist, but in uniform only. He would routinely use the phrase, "if there is one way to make an instructor really mad" in a loud voice for the entire class to hear while you stood next to him with whatever effort you had made. One learned quickly to not take things to Dr. Stock for evaluation unless you were having a fabulous day and were ready for the humiliation. It was all part of dental school.

By the time the end of my second year of dental school was coming to an end, I was seriously considering leaving the school and finding something entirely different to do. The problem was that since a very young age, I had never once thought about anything other than being a doctor and my pre-med (pre-dental) undergraduate years hadn't prepared me to pursue something else. To be honest, I was frustrated and frightened, unsure about what the next step might be. I had gone to the lab to work on some technique work one evening and a fourth-year student, Stan McAndrew, asked me how things were going. The extent to which I knew Stan was his name and that he was a fourth-year student. I had never had a conversation with him before. When I told him my sad tale, he thought for a moment, looked at me and said, "I think you might want to consider looking into Dr. Stock's project." I wasn't sure I'd heard him correctly and asked him to repeat what he'd said. When I realized that he had actually said what I thought he'd said, I nearly laughed in my misery and responded that I was certain that doing anything with Dr. Stock wasn't going to make things better for me. Stan only smiled and said, "You might be surprised." It's hard to remember how I decided to take the chance, but I believe it was Stan's sincerity and my desperation.

A few days later I ventured into Dr. Stock's office and was met with a warm and friendly smile from his secretary, Roseanne. I explained to her why I was there, and she could hardly stifle a little chuckle, and, in a forthright fashion, she said to me, "I imagine you have your doubts." Stunned by her candor, I couldn't help but admit she was correct while hoping that Dr. Stock wasn't within earshot. She explained to me that while Dr. Stock had a persona in the classroom, he had an alter-ego when he was outside of it. Heartened, I asked her to tell me more and she rolled out a story that was nearly unbelievable. Roseanne described how Dr. Stock, of his own volition, purchased used city buses and then, with his own money and his own energy, would gut them and convert them into mobile dental clinics. Once completed, he would drive them down to California's Central Valley each summer, and there, provide care for the children of the migrant workers who toiled in the fertile fields. Somehow this struck a chord in me, and I asked Roseanne for more details. She explained to me that the instructors on the project were not the school instructors, but rather the pedodontic graduate students. (*When I was in dental school, the specialty was called "pedodontics" and the specialists were called "pedodontists"*) They were there to provide encouragement and support to the volunteers. It was difficult to imagine that such a situation could exist, given my experiences in the school setting. When I asked others who had gone, they all agreed that it had been a very positive and rewarding thing for them. Whether it was my desperation or some unrecognized philosophy/skill/goal inside me, I told Roseanne a few days later that I wanted to be a part of it.

Having commuted from my home in Tucson, Arizona, to the Bay Area for the previous six years, I was well acquainted with the central valley. Traveling down Interstate 5 was a familiar route, and, as we approached the Merced and Visalia area, my excitement and nervousness grew. Much like entering dental school, I had no idea what was ahead of me. Pulling into the camp, as I eventually called it, I was struck by the commitment and the professionalism of the volunteers who had arrived well ahead of me. They set up the three buses, the panel truck that held all the supplies, and x-ray equipment. I was amazed by the remarkable simplicity of the operation. Dr. Stock had built the buses in such a way that they only required an electrical hookup and a garden hose for the water. All the equipment, which is considerable for a dental office, was built into the bus. That included a vacuum system for the suction units, a compressor for the air-driven hand pieces and the usual items such as dental chairs, lights and everything else one would expect to see upon entering a full-blown dental facility. I met the other volunteers, many of whom came from Santa Clara University, as well as the graduate students who would be both my instructors and, I hoped, my sources of encouragement. These young men were only three years older than I, but they seemed so much wiser. Experience in dentistry comes quickly and relentlessly and those three years had provided them with enough to afford them the confidence that I so sorely lacked. My hopes rose, but so did my heart rate. Would this be all right for me, or would it become my last gasp at finding a way into dentistry? The next day would be my first opportunity to find out and I felt ready.

As is usually the case in the central valley in the summer, the day dawned with sun, a blue sky and promises of a warm, if not hot, day. I did not wear a smock, but rather wore a short-sleeve shirt and a pair of shorts. I was hardly a clothes horse in those days on my limited budget, but it didn't matter at all—most of the other volunteers were either similarly dressed or in jeans. The director of the operation, Sophie, was a young, but experienced, woman who had been on the project for several years and on the first morning I noticed with both relief and some amusement that she treated me and the other greener than green dental students with some very matter-of-fact direction. There was no pandering but rather some clear directions about how the process would work. We would be far more on our own than we would be in the school setting, but that the graduate students would always be available if any problems arose. That final statement stuck in my mind since I was fairly certain there would be some problems!

Once the children arrived, the camp came alive with registrations, x-rays, charting and all of it happening with a remarkable efficiency and lacking any chaos. It was my first look at what a dental practice might be even though it was all happening outdoors, all with young patients and all by volunteer workers. I was impressed. Would I be able to measure up to this astonishing operation? My level of confidence was low and wasn't warranted to be any higher. After all, I had only seen one patient in my life and that was under the wing of a student one year ahead of me, so he could gently guide me through each step of treating another human being. This was hardly a curriculum vitae to give me cause for feeling confident or competent. To be honest, I can't clearly recall the first child I saw, but somehow, I made it through the visit, as did the child. I voicelessly said a small prayer of thanks that we both had survived. My second patient of the day, however, had an appointment that I can almost recall every agonizing detail.

Before describing that appointment, though, I must digress for the benefit of the reader to explain that dental training includes many admonitions about the sanctity of the dental pulp, which is the home to the nerve of the tooth as well as the blood supply. We are painstakingly taught about the depth of the enamel on various teeth, the depth of the underlying dentin and how to approach removal of the decay in such a way that we would never, ever fall into the pulp. It felt as though this was the dental equivalent for a medical student to let someone die. I believe all of us constantly felt nervous about the dreaded possibility of "hitting the pulp." Jumping ahead to my third year of dental school for a moment, this concern was so great that my very first solo patient in my life was (prophetically enough) a seven-year-old girl named Maria Crane. She was a nice girl who had a very small cavity on her upper right first permanent molar. My mania for not "hitting the pulp" was so intense that I must have called the instructor over a minimum of eight times to check my progress. I can recall Dr. Wing patiently telling me that I hadn't even gotten through the enamel yet! In other words, I had hardly begun. Maria, a model patient, endured this "care" that I was providing with no complaints. At the end of her three-hour appointment (yes, *THREE-HOUR* appointment) I had to place a temporary filling into the miniscule ditch I had dug into her tooth. Within a couple of years, this was a procedure I would complete start-to-finish within ten minutes. But…..I didn't hit the pulp!

Back to my second appointment on the mobile dental clinic bus. My second patient was a five- year-old girl whose name will forever be emblazoned in my memory bank. Luz Cordero was this bright-eyed girl's name and she walked in with an uncanny confidence far surpassing my own. She told me that she had a tooth that was bothering her and upon examination, it was obvious that the size of the cavity was, at that moment in my young career, the most monstrous one I had ever seen. I could understand why it was bothering her and was mildly surprised that she wasn't swollen or screaming in pain. She was neither. With the needle on my local anesthetic syringe wagging like a puppy-dog's tail, I successfully got her numb and placed all the paraphernalia into her mouth, that being the items that prevent patients from being able to talk to her/his dentist, even when questions are being asked.

Not too many readers would truly enjoy the details of how we dentists clean a tooth, but of course the well-known and equally dreaded "drills" are the primary instruments we have to accomplish this procedure. Hand instruments, such as our aptly named "spoon excavator" can also clean the decay, but they are less efficient and far slower—the latter being an aspect I actually appreciated. As I removed the decay form Luz's tooth, it just seemed to go on and on. I noticed the central valley heat was increasing and I literally felt the sweat on my forehead forming as I approached.....yes, the pulp. As carefully as possible, I worked my way around the periphery of the decayed area to lessen the chances of exposing the pulp, but in spite of my best efforts, I saw some blood coming from the tooth. It is not possible to find the words to adequately describe my horror. After all that training, I still managed to hit the pulp and felt the shame wash over me. I was already a raw nerve, but now that nerve had been seared and I realized that I needed help. I was in over my head. With fear and embarrassment, I called to one of the graduate students, expecting some form of humiliation that I had already experienced in my dental school classes. Dr. Guy Peters, one of the graduate students came in and asked how he could help. I swallowed, searching for the best way to confess my sin, and ultimately blurted out, "I hit the pulp." Dr. Peters, who ultimately became one of my most important mentors and good friends, looked me directly in the eye and said to me, "So?" This was an alternate universe. I had committed the ultimate sin and he only asked a one-word question. I apologized to him and, indirectly, to Luz and asked what I should do. Dr. Peters gently and confidently told me to do a pulpotomy on the tooth. At this point, I had had no training in pediatric dental procedures and had no idea what he had just said to me. My face obviously conveyed that to Guy as he suggested he "sit down and help for a moment." He was a god, he was brilliant, he was capable, and he was confident. Within moments he completed the procedure and then suggested a put a crown on the tooth. I asked if I could put the filling into the tooth behind the one being treated and asked if Guy wanted to show me the best way to do a crown since again, I had no idea. "Of course," was all he said and again, within moments, he completed the care for that tooth, turned Luz back over to me and left. By now Luz had a tear slowly rolling down her face and her eyebrows were knit, so I knew she was tired. I decided to step up the pace and get the filling done and soon, Luz, tears and all, was on her way. Failure was the only word I could think. My gamble to come to a positive environment and change my attitude toward the better had just resulted in my hitting the pulp and leaving the child crying. I wanted to cry myself. The rest of the day was a blur and over dinner, I felt as though I should just head back to San Francisco, pack up and look for something else to do with the rest of my life.

Morning dawned again with the sun, blue sky and the promise of another lovely day. Also, a good night's sleep had helped me set aside my misery and my self-deprecation. Dr. Peters also spoke with me a few moments about how that tooth needed the pulpotomy no matter how careful I had been and that it is a routine procedure. He was the first dentist to ever shed light on the concept that while one never tries to hit the pulp, it is ultimately the depth of the decay that will dictate the outcome, not the operator's carelessness. I appreciated his wisdom and his encouragement. I'm sure it was the foundation of what became a close friendship. I wanted to be like Guy, but I knew this day wasn't when that would happen.

Feeling better, I returned to the bus with a greater sense of self-worth and a willingness to do my best and accept that I couldn't be perfect, given my dearth of experience. Once again, the details of each child's visit are lost on me because the life-changing moment that occurred that day overshadowed any sense of guilt, ineptness or self-defeating words. I was wrapping up the appointment of a child when Sophie entered the bus and told me I had a patient who wanted to see me. By this time, I had seen about eight or ten children, so I couldn't imagine who it might be. As I turned to look toward the door, in walked Luz, her face glowing with a smile and her eyes twinkling. She walked right up to me and said, "I want you to be my dentist." Had I known the profound impact of that moment, I would doubtless have written every single detail into a journal, but the mere fact that I can still relive those words and her face tells me that even almost fifty years later, it was a seminal moment in my life that changed everything. I wasn't sure what to say in response to her simple words, but before I could compose those words or myself Luz told me that her tooth didn't hurt anymore and that she wanted me to fix more of her cavities. Lucky for both of us, she had no other monster cavities, and her second visit was the first fulfilling event in my dental career. Luz came back both of the next two days and wanted to show me her baby brother, who she hefted onto her hip much like a miniature mother. My interactions with Luz helped me realize that I did have a niche in dentistry, and it would be with children. The rest of the week on the mobile clinic flew by and I eagerly signed up for it again the following summer, although that is the story of another chapter.

Left: Luz right after she told me, "I want you to be my dentist."
Right: Luz at the mobile dental clinic bus with the 1973 version of me—hair and all.

Suddenly, dental school didn't seem quite so onerous. My vision for the future was clear and my goal became to complete all the requirements to obtain my dental degree. Once that was done, I could focus my complete attention on learning all I could about pediatric dentistry. I never knew what happened to Luz and it is difficult for me to envision her as a fifty-some year-old woman now, but her smiling face and her expression of trust in me will forever live in my memory bank of critical moments in my life. I think about all the moments that had to occur to bring me to that moment—Stan's comment, Roseanne's reassurance, Guy's gentle guidance,

Luz's pivotal role-- and I can only think that miracles do happen. If nothing else, it taught me to always keep my eyes, ears and heart open to all possibilities because you never know who will provide the spark. In my case, it was every one of those people, and it lit a fire under me.

CHAPTER 4

Άνοιξε το στόμα σου, Καλαμαρακία και ΡΟΤΖΕΡ

Once I was bitten by the pedodontics bug, I was ready to dig in as far as possible. As things turned out, Dr. Stock not only had buses in the central valley of California, but he had also created buses for Israel and Greece. On weekends during my third year of dental school, I volunteered to work on building yet another one for the country then known as Yugoslavia. Not being overly clever with many of the construction issues that needed to be completed, it was still another schooling process, but this one was entirely mechanical. I was amazed at the dedication and imagination it took to convert a bus into a dental clinic. My first time on the mobile dental clinics, I simply stepped into a completed bus and somehow failed to understand how it had been transformed. Several others were involved in this project, and it was with quite a flush of excitement and accomplishment when we first plugged in the power, hooked up the water, and found that everything was working perfectly. As with many lessons in life, I had no way of knowing that this would be still another key moment in my long-term plans for my life. I largely worked on it because, by doing so, Dr. Stock would pay my way to participate in the Greek project. Since my family's paternal roots were directly from Greece, I was more than enthusiastic to go. On my student budget, I couldn't dream of purchasing an airfare, so the weekends of work on the bus were both educational and fiscally necessary.

I had visited Greece three times previously because of my time at Stanford University. I was fortunate to live in Vienna, Austria for a year and a half and, while there, spent two Christmas seasons and one very hot week in May in and around Athens. I had relatives there and visited them each time. Much to his distress, my father never taught my brothers or me Greek when we were children, primarily because my mother was not Greek. It was not the language of the household. The summer before my first trip, I bought a teach-yourself-Greek book since there were no CD's, DVD's or even cassette tapes available at that time. That summer I worked at a copper mine in southern Arizona since it was the best-paying job I could get. It paid $2.42 per hour, but at that time (1968) a loaf of bread cost 25 cents, and gasoline was 20-24 cents per gallon, depending on the stage of the gas wars. I felt as if I was making big money. One of the unexpected, but very helpful, aspects of working in the summer was that the regular miners took vacation time to be with their children. As a result, college students, like me, could occasionally get overtime by working a double-shift or, even better, could step into a different job to escape the mind-numbing work that defined my job. I normally spent eight hours per day with a garden hose in my hand washing down the floor of the processing mill when one of the gigantic mills became too heavy from the ore being crushed. Rather than allowing the motors to burn out, the entire contents would be intentionally spilled onto the floor. It was my job to wash it all off the floor. Occasionally, I needed a front-end loader to get the process started, as the contents of one mill covered the equivalent a very large living room. One of the jobs that became available because of my "seniority" was tailings pond operator. That job, much to my great surprise, literally involved a total of twenty minutes of work per eight-hour shift. I had to ask my foreman three times to make sure this was correct, as my work ethic on every job I ever had was to give the company its money's worth through my efforts. It was explained to me that the importance of the work was so vital that there could be nothing extraneous to distract me from the vital measurements I was to take. I measured the specific gravity of the tailings coming from the mill to the ponds where the worthless dirt, having had its copper removed, was simply dumped into the desert in enormous heaping piles. I had to measure the specific gravity to ensure that the tailings would flow through the pipes without clogging them, but still with the minimum amount of water, given the volume necessary. While it was true that I would drive the pickup I was given out to the tailing ponds to also make sure things were running well, I essentially had seven and a half hours per shift to study my Greek. It was hardly enough. While with my relatives, I did my best to communicate, but the phrase I heard most often was "ti lei?" That means, "What did he say?" One of my relatives (it's always difficult to determine exactly how people are truly related in Greece) told me in his heavily accented English, "Grigori, you keela zee Grick lahnguage." He was right.

It was quite a shift for me when I went with my group to the mobile clinic bus in Greece because even with my rudimentary and woefully inadequate Greek, I was clearly far ahead of all the others. They didn't speak a word. I felt like Demosthenes. I would teach the others how to say all the crucial commands to the children, such as μι κουνεσάι (pronounced mee koon-YES-eh" meaning "don't move" or άνοιξε το στόμα σου (pronounced AH-neck-seh toe STOMA-soo) or "open your mouth." Since there are really so few phrases used during a dental appointment with children, my confidence grew. We provided care for the children of migrant workers, but in this case, it was somewhat the reverse of what I'd done in California. Many Greeks would migrate to other countries, such as Germany, to find work. In the summertime they would send their children back to the motherland to attend a camp that imbued them with the Greek culture that was lacking in their adopted country. This was an opportunity to enjoy themselves with their fellow Greek youngsters and to learn games, dances, stories, and many other aspects of their heritage. I found it to be fun to roam around the camp myself. Even if my understanding of the words was poor at best, the smiles and laughter of the children was the universal language that couldn't be missed.

As for the dentistry, I had a full year of experience at this point, which increased both my knowledge and my skills. Working on the children was not the harrowing experience I had had during that first time in the Central Valley. As with any skill, the repetition of the words to the children became second nature and I found myself wishing that I could have my dear relatives as dental patients so that they could at last hear something understandable coming from their American cousin. Many of the children were amused by it, a few were fearful of being "at the dentist," but, as I ultimately learned throughout my career, once they realized that a dental appointment was something they could not only handle, but also master, they happily boarded the bus for their second or third visits. When I told them my name was Grigori Psaltis, they lit up as though they had found a long-lost friend. It brought out the greatest Hellenic pride in me that I had ever experienced. When I shared my name with them, they often opened a conversation that was unintelligible to me, but once again, the shared smiles and hugs spanned the gap in most instances. I felt a sense of the triumphant return to the land from which my grandparents had emigrated more than eighty years prior, and I wondered what they would have thought about a grandson spending a summer providing care for other Greek emigrants. I was sure they would have been proud.

The team was made up of a University of Michigan dental student, Larry (and his wife), a dental hygiene student, Marianne, from Fresno, two volunteers from Santa Clara University, (Caitlin and Brad) and a faculty advisor, Dr. Roger Peterson. It was amusing to tape our "Greek" names onto our shirts so the children would know who we were because some of the names simply did not have a Greek equivalent. Those names would be spelled out phonetically, at times with memorable results. For example, there is no "j" sound in Greek per se, so that when Roger had his name on his shirt, it was necessary to use a diphthong that most closely resembled the sound. In Greek that was a combination of the letters tau and zeta. The combination, just as in a word like spritzer, at least gave the children an idea. It was also entertaining that the Greek letter for the English "r" is rho, and, when written in the capital letter form, looks exactly like an English "P." As a result of these linguistic oddities, Roger's name, when spelled out on his shirt became POTZEP. Needless to say, we all embraced the idea of calling Dr. Peterson by the English phonetic spelling, which came out "pot zep." A good sport, he laughed along with us. It was not only Roger's name, though, that provided entertainment. The Greek letter "B," or beta, is not pronounced with the same explosive sound that the English letter "b" has. Instead, it is actually pronounced with a beginning "v" sound, so that it is properly pronounced "vee-tah." Since some Greek words are simply imported directly from our language, more adjustments were needed.

When we wanted to go somewhere for a beer, we would head to a bar. There is no Greek letter that phonetically gives the word its proper opening sound, so it was again a diphthong that did the trick. To make an English "b" sound, one needs to combine the Greek letters "mu" and "pi." Recalling that the final "r" in Greek looks like a "p" in English, the sign at a bar would be MPAP. I'm sure the Greeks could easily provide equivalent stories about words in English, so I never felt as if I was making fun of their language. It was merely a laugh for us.

On the weekends that we had free, we spent time sightseeing and relaxing, often by the sea. The universal food stands provided us with a variety of Greek goodies with which I was already familiar, but the others in the group were not. Once again, as the resident "expert," I could scan the menu and explain what *tiropitas* were, what was in *moussaka*, extol the virtues of *koulouria* and *avgolemono* soup as well as other delicacies. I loved my important role as food educator as well as eating foods that were both familiar and a treat to me. The things I ordered with the greatest frequency were *kalamarakia* and *karpouzi*. When my plate would be served to me, the watermelon was familiar to all, but in 1974 with a young crew, not everyone was familiar with fried squid. Since I always ordered the *kalamarakia*, it ensured that I would be served the small squids that were essentially intact. Rather than the large circles of squid that one may get at a restaurant, these little creatures still looked exactly like a miniature octopus or squid. The others found little to like about this plate and eagerly asked what else was on the menu. From my standpoint, it didn't matter, as I was reluctant to share my selection with people who didn't appreciate its wonderment. It was about ten days or so into our stay that someone finally took my suggestion to at least "give it a try." The reaction was immediate as the brave one's eyes popped open, a smile spread across the face and a five-star review ensued. Once the taboo was surmounted, others jumped on board and for the final couple of weeks of the project, I was both pleased and a bit smug to hear the orders for "*kalamarakia* and *karpouzi*" going into the kitchen for several of the volunteers.

One of my many Greek patients, Agathi

Since I was only at the end of my third year of dental school and hadn't had my rotation through the pedodontics department yet, I often wonder to what extent my philosophy of treating children grew out of the fact that the first young patients I ever treated were all foreign language speakers. Not able to always communicate verbally in a fluid fashion, it was necessary to do so with an unspoken manner including facial expressions, body language and a confidence that I frankly lacked initially but, at some point, embraced. It has always been my belief that the most important part of pediatric dentistry is the *relationship* and, without it, the *treatment* was never possible. It was a blessing to develop and hone my skills with children who may not have understood everything I was *saying*, but clearly understood the *compassion* with which I cared for them.

SECTION TWO- LEARNING THE ROPES

It's called the *practice* of dentistry, not the *I-know-everything-about-it* of dentistry

Nobody sits down at a piano at Carnegie Hall for the first lesson. Like every other skill, it takes time, effort, concentration, and practice to hone one's skills for anything to be mastered. In order to be an effective dentist, one must have the technical skills to do the procedures that define the physical part of the work. Occasionally people would mention to me that "you dentists are all such perfectionists," as if this were something bad. To reflect perspective back to them, I would reply, "Yes, we are, but when your child comes into the office, I can certainly let my perfectionism go." That one phrase speaks volumes about why dentists are the way they are. In fact, the profession draws technophiles who enjoy all the gadgets involved with restoring people's mouths to excellent health. When I see my own dentist, I want him to be on his game—no B- work in my mouth, please.

Like many professions, dentistry is constantly changing. From the early days of no masks, no assistants, and stand-up dentistry, the profession has evolved into an efficient health care system that employs many people and provides care that may have been unimaginable when I sat upright in Dr.

Wainright's dental chair in 1957. It all requires practice and learning, but never more so than in the early years of one's career. When one is fresh and green out of dental school, the knowledge a new dentist possesses is remarkably thin. This is something that we only discover as time passes, and we notice that fillings that previously took us hours now require only minutes. Materials change, equipment changes and, as a result, we also change.

If there were two significant gaps that existed in our skill sets upon graduation, I would put communication at the very top and, in the second place for most of us, confidence. The dental school setting, in retrospect, was a four-year program that I now view as the opportunity to learn what a perfect procedure looked like so that as we entered into our own practices, we would have a picture in our mind of "how things should be." In working toward that vision, though, it was not an easy path for our egos. Like all other students of a profession, the people are neither lacking in intelligence or in self-motivation. At times it was difficult to not feel stupid and/or inept. A few of my classmates did not seem to suffer from these afflictions, but as the son of a man who would look at my report card, see seven A's and one B and only comment on the latter, I was exquisitely sensitive to anything with the slightest sniff of failure. I had been programmed.

The journey from dental school to being a successful, confident, and happy dentist was a bumpy one, but also a necessary one. I learned as I went, which ultimately became my actual dental education. I learned each day, was humbled at times, proud at times and uncertain at times. I had to find out that being a dentist is also being human. Not too many humans I know are perfect and being a part of a profession in which perfection is the standard essentially leaves its members with only one direction to go. I'm grateful for each step I took, the people who supported and taught me, and the growth I experienced so that my career became a blessing. This section is the brief story of the significant phases of my development.

CHAPTER 1

A not-so-reserved reservist

Sadly, I have very little to say about my two-year residency in pedodontics. What I can say is that in 1975, when I graduated from dental school, the American Dental Association had some remarkable statistics about dental demographics. Those statistics proved that the specialists in the field of children's dentistry were not only the worst paid among all dental specialists, but that they earned less income than the general dentists of the United States. I have always maintained that the only people going into the field at that time were either crazy or passionate. At times I wondered myself, although I put those concerns to rest long ago.

In short, I will say that the best things that happened to me in my residency were one, that it gave me the certification to declare myself a specialist and two, that I met Dr. Mel Barkley, one of the kindest and most patient instructors I had in my years at UCSF. Beyond that, I felt that I was largely on my own with self-education. One may argue that all students are existentially on their own, but most of my years in college-level and post-graduate training had significantly more structure than those two years. While I did manage to make an important connection for the future, my lasting impression of my two years is that they elapsed, and I obtained my certification. I will leave it at that.

When I entered dental school, my dentist brother advised me that upon graduation I would have three options into the future. I could open my own practice, for which I would be quite unprepared, I could become an associate in an established practice, which was often a less than ideal relationship, or I could join the military. He had done the latter and fully enjoyed his two years in the U.S. Navy. It made sense to me, and so I voluntarily signed up for the reserves. Many people think that the military pays for the professional training, but only a few of the students enjoy this benefit. For me, it was merely a way to ensure my future and to gain time "in rank" during my dental training. Our monthly reserve meetings were lunches around a table with an oral surgery instructor, who had retired from the Navy, leading the minimal conversations. I also spent a month at Newport, Rhode Island, learning how to be a naval officer. It was hardly as intense as the dental training, but necessary to know about the uniform, the formalities of going onto a ship, and other naval matters.

Luckily, when I planned to enter my specialty training, I contacted the naval authorities and asked if it might be possible to defer my two years of active duty until I had completed my residency. Dental care for dependents, as all non-military family members are called, had not always been provided. Realizing the morale problem of the sailors and officers stationed at "foreign shores," the navy adjusted this policy and began a program to enhance the bases located in Italy, Spain, Iceland, the Philippines, Guam, and Japan with schools as well as other necessities for the families of the active-duty personnel. The result of this was that suddenly children's dentists were needed, and my request was granted. I remember putting in the call to Captain Gray, who was the detailer (the officer in charge of assigning duty stations) explaining that I had completed my training. Captain Gray told me that he had three possible duty stations available for me. Eagerly, I listened to the options. Guantanamo Bay, Cuba, was first on his list. In 1977 it was not the home for incarcerated terrorists, but it was a tiny enclave on the island of Cuba and getting off the base was not easy with Fidel Castro in charge of things. No thank you. Second up was Twentynine Palms, a marine flight station in the middle of the Mojave Desert in southern California, deemed so remote that the navy did not expect any of the personnel to make the lengthy drive into a point of civilization for care of any sort. Once again, this was not my idea of a cultural experience, and I suddenly had a gnawing feeling of concern in my gut. Finally, the third choice was the Naval Regional Dental Center in Yokosuka, Japan. It took less than a moment to say yes to option three. I love travel, am stimulated by living in foreign countries, and I already knew the commanding officer of the dental facility there. Captain Whitely had been my commanding officer at Treasure Island Naval Base on the small island in San Francisco Bay below the Bay Bridge. When the navy changed its reserve meeting format to a day at a naval facility to treat patients, I was assigned to the nearest base for my monthly drills—Treasure Island. Captain Whitely had asked me to prepare some in-service training sessions during my days there, which proved to be another turning point in my professional life, although I didn't realize it at the time.

Within weeks, I was flying on a military flight to Yokota Air Base where I was met by my sponsors, Rollie and Deidre Dade. The navy cared for its own and when a new person reported for duty in Japan, one of the other dentists would take the "newbie" under his arm to guide him on things that he should have learned in Newport. It was a good thing, since I deplaned the aircraft without my "cover." I apparently missed that lesson in Newport, but one must always wear a hat, which is "cover" in military language. I walked up to Rollie and Deidre bare headed. They proved to be wonderful sponsors, showing me many facets of my new life and providing smiling and welcoming faces. My first housing was at the Navy Lodge, the usual starting point for new arrivals. I was told that the new Executive Officer (XO) of the clinic, Captain Howell, had also arrived that day, and I thought it might be good to invite him to dinner to get to know him. This was another breach of military etiquette. I clearly had lots to learn.

My arrival at the dental clinic for my first day was spent filling out the mandatory forms and meeting the people already stationed there. This was my first taste of how children's dentists were a more-than-welcome addition to a clinic. The relief was palpable once the other men (there were no female dentists at that time) found out someone had arrived who could deal with the kids. There was a children's dentist, Harvey, already at the base, but his departure was nearing and apparently people feared the prospect of seeing patients under five feet tall. While Harvey was still working, I was told to treat the active-duty personnel, my final instances of looking into adult mouths, until Harvey's tour of duty was over.

Not everyone was as enthused about my arrival, though. Captain Howell, who was unique in that he was a graduate of the U.S. Naval Academy and was navy through and through, pulled me aside and said, in no uncertain words, that "the mission of the Navy dental corps is to treat the active-duty personnel." I shook my head in understanding and replied, "Yes, sir, and I am here to take care of the children of the active-duty personnel." He did not smile or flinch. He also did not change his opinion and, to make that clear to me, he looked me in the eye with a serious face and said, "The mission of the Navy dental corps is to treat the active-duty personnel." I wasn't sure what to make of that since Captain Gray had assured me that my specialty skills would be needed at the base. Not to worry, though, as Captain Whitely stepped in and over-rode the XO's vision by saying that I was there to treat children. I didn't feel it sat well with Captain Howell. I also knew that Captain Whitely had two children living on the base, which may have helped my cause. Either way, I was officially the pedodontist of the base. In spite of my thin training program, I realized that I knew far more than any other dentist there about my specialty and that I was also the only one who was willing to treat children.

The rest was easy. Since all appointments for the clinic had to be made at the front desk, I knew that the volume of patients I wanted to see would create a problem. As a result, I requested a different room that was large enough for two dental chairs and my own phone line. In return, I would book all the appointments, follow-up with every family and create a priority list so that the children in greatest need could be seen first. I was mildly surprised to have my request granted and from that point, I was able to truly learn how to be a children's dentist. I was the end of the line, so if there was something that needed to be done, I would find a way to handle it. There was no internet, no cell phones, and no fellow pediatric specialists, so I learned very quickly to use my best judgment and get the results I wanted. This included use of orthodontic appliances and all forms of restorative care--fillings, etc. In short, it was my genuine residency.

It didn't take long before my request bore fruit. The dental assistants at the base were Japanese women because of the SOFA (Status of Forces Agreement), which stated that any position on the base that could be filled by a Japanese national would be filled by a Japanese national. I had the very good fortune of working with Hanako, a relentless worker and tremendous supporter of my work.

Hanako with Lt. Psaltis

The dental unit in my room was a standard pole-mounted piece of equipment, but the critical parts—the light, the suction, the air-water syringe and the hand pieces—could all swivel sufficiently that I could see two children at once. I built my own dental "benches" at the navy woodshop and soon the number of procedures I was producing far outstripped any other dentist in the clinic. This wasn't because I was a red-hot who wanted to get promoted faster. It was simply because I wanted to learn as much as possible. Hanako would be doing a dental cleaning on one side of the pole while I was doing an examination on the other side. In keeping with my unusual tradition of seeing children of a different ethnicity, having begun my career with Hispanic and then Greek children, I found that Hanako was often helpful when a child who primarily spoke Japanese came in. It spurred me on to learn enough of the language to handle most of the cases in their native tongue. While Captain Howell continued to scowl about the fact that I wasn't seeing active-duty personnel, I knew that the numbers I was producing made the clinic look good.

One of my most compelling lessons, though, came at some risk. CINC-PAC-FLEET stood for Commander in Chief of the Pacific Fleet, a position held by an Admiral. There is both an aura about Admirals as well as a profound respect for them since it appears nearly impossible to obtain that lofty title without a spotless record. Captain Whitely came into my office one day and told me that a new CINC-PAC-FLEET had been assigned to the base and that I should contact the family and get his children right into my office. It was at that moment that I realized that my focus must always be for the children and that I needed to advocate for them. As directed by my commanding officer, I contacted the admiral's wife and had a delightful conversation with her. She told me she had two sons, and I asked her what their dental status was. She said that they'd just had check-ups and needed no fillings. I took a deep breath and told her that my CO had requested that I get the boys right in to my office, but that there was a waiting list of other children who were in need of significant care. I added that it might be up to two months before I could see her children based on my waiting list, but that I would see them whenever she wanted. There was a pause on the phone, and I feared I had just committed yet another military faux pas. After that worrisome moment, she told me that she was glad I was seeing the children who needed the care and that her boys would be "just fine" to wait for a couple of months. I was relieved and immediately grasped that I was not a genuine naval officer. I was a reservist. The career navy dentists were called "regulars," which I supposed made me an irregular. Regardless, it was clear to me that the children, themselves, do not have a higher or lower rank. Their parents have those titles. For my patients, need came first without consideration of their parents' status. It was a lesson I carried throughout my entire career. When Captain Whitely asked me if I'd contacted the admiral's wife, I told him that it was all handled. Fortunately, his duties as commanding officer must have kept him busy enough to never ask the admiral about his children's appointments. My guess would have been that the admiral, himself, would not have known since matters of that sort were usually handled by the mothers.

The other major event during my three-year stint in Japan was that during my time there, I was literally the only American-trained pedodontist in all of Japan. Captain Whitely, having seen my in-service presentations while at Treasure Island, felt it would be helpful to the dentists at other naval bases to get more training, since no other base had a children's specialist. This opened the door for me to develop an enormous library of clinical photographs that would become essential to my future speaking career. I was flown around Japan, sometimes in a helicopter, to Sasebo, on Kyushu; Iwakuni Marine Base, near Hiroshima; and Atsugi Air Station, the home of the planes that went out to sea on aircraft carriers. Along with my friend, Tim Foster, the orthodontist at the base, I spoke at the Tri-services dental conference at Yokota Air Force Base. It was very fortuitous that I had the opportunity to develop my speaking skills and to learn enough to make certain that I was teaching procedures that were up to date. Little did I know at the time that years later it would parlay into a secondary career as a speaker at dental conferences that took me all over the world.

Considering that I was only a reservist, I know my years in the U.S. Navy were fruitful, educational, and fulfilling. Without those years, I'm not sure I could have launched a private practice as effectively and with as much confidence as I eventually did.

On a final note, near the end of my tour of duty in Japan I was informed that I had been in rank of Lieutenant long enough that I was being promoted to Lieutenant Commander. When I was officially given my new status, a small ceremony was held in Captain Whitely's office, and I was moved by the fact that my new LCDR pins for my khaki uniform were given to me by none other than Captain Howell. I hope it was more than the numbers of procedures that inspired him to do that act of kindness.

CHAPTER 2

A silver platter that I tarnished

It's difficult enough to open a private practice when you know where you want to establish your roots and are already living there. When I was in the navy in Japan, nothing was farther from my thoughts, both literally and figuratively, than my next step after my tour of duty. Most of my life I have been a planner, typically laying out the next step so that I could be prepared. However, sleeping on a futon that rested on a tatami mat somehow removed me from the reality that when I headed home, I'd need to have a landing spot. Some call it fate, some call it karma, and still others call it a coincidence. In my mind, I have more recently referred to magical moments in my life as the universe taking care of me. And so it was when my next step presented itself on a silver platter.

As a student I had been aware of some of the San Francisco Bay Area practitioners and had the seed of an idea about how I wanted to spend my life. When my aunts mentioned to me about "having a family life," I realized that the pattern set up by two pediatric dentists in Alameda, California, might be just what I wanted. I had never heard of two dentists sharing a single practice, but that was exactly what Drs. Olmstead and Pearle had done. They decided that each would work three days a week, Olmstead on Monday through Wednesday, and Pearle Thursday through Saturday.

It was almost unimaginable to me that this would work, and yet the two of them had been in practice this way for several years. Their model became my goal.

I definitely pondered this during my Navy years, but I still couldn't figure out where I might best accomplish it. I put my energies into learning the skills and decided to let the future take care of itself. Everything else in my life had worked out well, so why not a practice location? In a most unexpected turn of events, I received a letter in Japan from my former instructor, Dr. Mel Barkley. Much to my shock as well as pleasure, he explained to me that he and his partner, Dr. Don Thomison, decided I might be the perfect fit to join them in their longstanding practice in Sacramento, California. It took some time to let this sink in. Dr. Barkley was one of my favorite instructors and while he was not exactly warm and fuzzy, he was supportive, knowledgeable and, to an extent, rather businesslike. In his letter he outlined the plan to have me come into the practice on a part-time basis with the possibility of buying in as a partner if all worked out well. The Barkley-Thomison practice was the one that many pediatric dentists wished they could emulate or, even better, be a part of. I was stunned by my good fortune and planned a trip to have an on-site visit and interview. Dr. Thomison had never met me, and both of the men wanted a face-to-face meeting. I was more than willing.

As with many military adventures, this required a unique means of getting there. The closest air force base, Yokota Air Base, was the place from which the "hops" departed. The definition of a "hop" was a military flight on which one may travel without specific orders to do so. In civilian terms, it would be called a space available situation. I went to Yokota, signed in for any flight that could take me to California, and took a seat. After quite a while, an air force non-commissioned officer approached me and asked if I would like to be a courier. Not knowing what that might be, I asked and was told that I would be given a sealed packet, sign for it, agree to keep it on my person for the entire flight and give it to the person named on the envelope after seeing his military identity card. I told him I could do that, and he said that he could get me onto a flight within fifteen minutes, but I needed to be in uniform. Luckily, I had one, so I dashed to the restroom, quickly changed into my dress blues and hustled back to the desk. The packet was given to me, and I was escorted across the tarmac to a cargo plane and told my seat was ready. As it turned out, I had the only seat in the entire cargo bay, which was big enough to carry almost anything I could imagine. That alone was interesting enough, but to add to the occasion, the seat faced backwards and when the engines fired up, all lights went off so that I was sitting in the dark. I have no recollection of how long we had been in the air before a man with a flashlight approached me and asked if there was anything he could do for me. I told him it would be good to get warm and have some light, so he asked me if I wanted to join him in the cockpit. Who would turn down an offer like that? The young man in the pilot's seat seemed younger than I might have imagined, so when I asked him how long he'd been a pilot, he smiled and said that he wasn't the pilot. The plane was flying on autopilot, giving me an appreciation for the power of automation, even at 30,000 feet in the air. I probably spent an hour or two allowing myself to be educated and entertained before I was told it was time to return to the cargo bay. I managed to doze off, and, when I awoke, we were only an hour or so out of Travis Air Force Base in California. Just as advertised, the person whose name appeared on the packet was waiting for me. He was an enlisted man and snapped off a sharp salute, received the packet, and I was free to go. I never expected to have an experience in an airplane cockpit when I was in the US Navy, but it was a reminder to always be ready for anything.

Dr. Barkley picked me up and took me to his home, where I was greeted by his hospitable wife as well as Dr. and Mrs. Thomison. All four were welcoming and enthusiastic to talk to me about my time in Japan and my future plans. An aura of being unreal coursed through me although the wine and dinner were real enough. I toured the office and met some of the staff members and had to keep reminding myself that all of this was real, wonderful and, potentially, my future. We discussed the business plan, and, when my wife at that time traveled to Sacramento after my visit, we decided it would be an opportunity that we simply couldn't resist. The paperwork started flying back and forth across the Pacific Ocean as my stint in the Navy drew to a close and suddenly the future that had seemed so hard to imagine came into focus. I was excited. I was also nervous.

When I finally arrived in Sacramento and set up house it was time to go to work and get paid for each procedure I completed. Nobody in the practice put any pressure on me to "produce" so that I could transition into a civilian practice. There were enough differences from my military arrangement that resetting my brain on insurance forms, informed consent, parents' questions, and other nuances already challenged me. These were some of the things that had never been a part of my practice in the navy, and it helped me understand a bit more why many prefer a career in the military. It is less complicated in many administrative ways. However, the biggest change for me was that in spite of the confidence I had garnered during my three years of active duty, I was now in a fishbowl with others watching me. That's not to say that they were literally staring at me, but with the open-bay concept of six chairs in a single room, anything I said or did for a patient could be heard and seen by anyone in the room. It was daunting. Both Mel and Don had been practicing for many years and carried the air of confidence that it would now take me a while to regain. The dental assistants, all of whom were supportive of me in all ways, were accustomed to working with two men whose experience and demeanor were enough to warrant respect, if not admiration. I still had to earn that.

I recall having a patient in the chair and I wasn't able to control his behavior. I wondered if it was because military children were more disciplined or that I had lost my touch. Either way I retreated into the private office I shared with the doctor not in the building that day and felt a wave of disappointment wash over me. After so many heady years of volunteering on the dental buses and then being the king of pediatric dentistry at the Naval Regional Dental Center in Yokosuka, Japan, I had been taken down a notch by a child. Or so I thought. Certain that the staff felt some sense of my shortcomings, I felt cowed. One of the many gifts I received from those two men was their reassurances. It was Don who told me that even after his many years of experience he still had children who were challenging, if not unmanageable. His words meant more to me than I'm sure he could imagine.

My time in Sacramento taught me many things. These two men explained their business philosophy, and it stayed with me for my entire career.

They told me that they put all their energy into success, but they always planned for failure. They taught me about contracts, conditions of employment, how to run an ethical practice, and how to enjoy the work more than the money, just to name a few. Unfortunately, it also taught me that work and home are not always in perfect alignment. After a fairly short time (about four months) my wife surprised me by saying that she couldn't live in Sacramento. Stunned, I suggested numerous options, none of which allayed her concerns. Having to choose between my commitment to her and my commitment to Don and Mel was the most difficult moment of my life. For me, it was Scylla or Charybdis and either way I knew I would be hurt badly.

The four of us went to lunch and I had to tell these wonderful men that I had to leave their practice. They, too, suggested several ideas, such as meeting more people or spending more time doing all there was to do in the city, but nothing sold the plan. I offered to stay for my one-year contractual commitment, and it was Don who told me that I should just leave now. He was right and I knew it, but inside I was dying. I'm sure this was not the sort of failure for which they had planned, and I felt that I had betrayed them.

A few days after our lunch, we packed up a U-Haul with the help of some dear friends and moved ourselves to Olympia, Washington, which had won out over Roseburg, Oregon; Coeur d' Alene, Idaho; and Puyallup, Washington; as the place I'd put down deep roots and open a practice of my own. While it ultimately turned out well for me in every way, it still leaves a mark on my soul that these two marvelous mentors were left with regrouping again and having to explain to staff, parents, children, and their community about why their associate had departed after a mere four months. The silver platter had been tarnished.

CHAPTER 3

Against some odds

It was only appropriate that moving to the Evergreen State further clarified that I was as green as a leaf in terms of having my own practice. In spite of the positive and educational experience with Mel and Don, I was naïve and concerned about my ability to create and run a practice. At this point my experience was primarily in the military, and it bore no resemblance to a civilian practice that required licenses, permits, supplies, and a business savvy that I was lacking. On the bright side, my enthusiasm offset many of those shortcomings so that I was eager to do whatever necessary to make my practice a success.

Even though I had no family, no friends, and no contacts in Olympia, I was confident that the opportunity in the city was too much to pass. I had met with several of the local dentists as well as a dental sales representative, all of whom said that the city needed a second pediatric dentist. The only one in town, Jonah Carlton, was so busy that he was booked months in advance. He also had stopped seeing public assistance patients, and the local family dentists had no place to send them other than to a pediatric practice thirty miles north in Tacoma. My sense was that as long as I didn't do something terribly wrong, it would be a golden opportunity to replace the silver one I just left.

The first order of business was deciding where to locate in town. I looked at several possible spots and ultimately felt the best one would be on Lilly Road, which was known in Olympia as "doctors' row." The new hospital had been built there and the street was lined with offices of doctors and dentists, but, more importantly, it was a known location throughout the region because of the hospital. Since referrals would be coming from as far as 100 miles away, I thought it was smart to locate on a street already familiar with the people in the broader area. The office space was the second side of an existing dental building and was entirely unfinished other than the exterior walls. This left me with the chance to construct exactly what I thought would work well for me. I was in contact with the dental supply companies to determine what I would require, and I began the process of meeting as many local dentists as possible to let them know I was in town and ready to accept all referrals, including public assistance.

Not so obvious to me was the financing. I did my homework and came to a figure of $100,000 that would suffice my needs to complete the construction, purchase the supplies, and still give myself some leeway for my own personal expenses. In today's world, when a new dentist might require up to six to eight times that amount, it still felt like a massive debt to incur. I applied to five banks for the loan with the help of my CPA, James Streeter. He was possibly the only man I ever met who was more fiscally conservative than my father, but I credit him with much of the early success I had in my practice. He assembled a loan proposal for me that was far beyond anything I might have imagined, and, without it, I may never have gotten started. I presented my proposal to each of the five banks in hopes of being able to decide which would give me the best rate. Once again, optimism far outweighed realism. Of the five banks, two of them turned me down outright, never even considering my proposal. Two of the others told me that my proposal would need to be seen by the "home office," meaning Seattle. Even in my naiveté I could read between the lines. This was a polite, but somewhat evasive "no." Suddenly it occurred to me that my plan was in serious peril. I had walked away from a sure thing to pursue my dream elsewhere and, without the financial backing of a bank, the dream was dead. To say that I entered the fifth and final bank quite nervously would be one of the great understatements of this book. I was escorted into the office of the bank vice-president, Don Harrington. I would love a video of that meeting. Knowing that I was facing the final chance, my voice probably squeaked as I introduced myself and began my little spiel. "Hi," I started, "my name is Greg Psaltis, and I am here in Olympia to open a dental practice for children." Before I could get another word out, Don interrupted me and said the precise words I most wanted to hear. "We're going to take care of you," he stated rather simply. As a lifelong runner, my heart rate is normally somewhere in the mid 50 beats per minute range. Walking into this meeting, I'm sure it must have been closer to 150 and, when Don's words escaped his mouth, it dropped drastically. It took a moment for it to sink in fully since I had been so worried about the possibility that the risk I had taken leaving Sacramento would end up with a devastating failure. When I regained my composure, I thanked him profusely. He explained that a local dentist was one of the bank's board of directors and he had told Don about the dire need for another kids' dentist. Apparently, that secured the loan.

Historically, 1981 was the year that the price of crude oil doubled. I am not an economist, so I don't really know the causes and effects of the science. What I did understand, though, was that inflation was running rampant and the economy wasn't doing all that well. Until the next moment, all of those numbers and reports felt rather removed from my own life experience, but Don quickly gave me a dose of reality. "We've written up your loan," Don said, "for the $100,000 you requested, and it will be at the rate of 21%." A desperate man does not argue, and the impact of the loan rate had far less impact on me than the approval of my application. It was the financial support from the bank that enabled me to begin my serious planning. My loyalty to Don was complete. Any time he moved on to a new bank, I followed. He became the latest in the series of key people in my life.

As I continued the promotion of my brand-new practice, I encountered several dentists who told me that they felt sorry for me to be opening at such a "difficult time." The theme that ran through these lamentations was that the economy was so bad that many people were not accepting treatment plans but deferring them out of concern for what was happening in the financial world. These portents of doom didn't do much to boost my morale, but now committed, I knew I simply had to keep moving forward and letting things unfold as they might. All I could do was continue to do my best. It didn't take long to discover one of the many gifts of being a pediatric dentist. I now refer to my specialty as the recession-proof specialty. I learned that if a family has limited funds available for medical or dental care, and a parent needs a filling and a child needs a filling, it is the child who will invariably get the treatment completed. I pondered this in terms of the stories I had heard from other dentists about their difficulties in getting adults to accept treatment plans. Yet again, I felt fortunate to have chosen my field.

Treatment room of my first office

To keep costs down, I personally constructed the waiting room furniture, the dental "benches" for the treatment area and the assistant carts. This gave me plenty to do while construction was being done on the space itself. Finally, in October of 1981, I opened my own practice with one dental assistant as my employee. The first patient I saw that day was a teenager and, ironically, the care she needed was a root canal on a permanent molar. It was not lost on me that root canals were among the many procedures that nudged me into pediatrics. It was the first and only root canal I ever performed in my private practice career. As the saying goes, desperate times….. It was a most unlikely way to open my Olympia career. It was not the only unusual aspect of that first-ever patient visit. When performing a root canal, one of the steps involves using bleach. While reaching for another instruments, I accidentally knocked the small cup of bleach over and watched it spill onto the brand-new rug, leaving a permanent stain that reminded me for five years about my first patient. Had I written a prediction of the practice's opening, this scenario would not have been in the top five hundred possibilities.

The practice grew quickly, and I felt better each day with its progress. After my five-year lease had expired, I bought an adjacent property and had my own building constructed. This allowed me to expand the number of chairs as well as accommodate my growing patient population. The story of the practice itself would fill another book, but it is not my intention to spend so much time on the business aspect of my career. I would only add to this brief history that I began my career at a time at which neither masks nor gloves were worn, much to the horror of the current generation of dentists. I also opened the practice using a paper appointment book and paper billing forms that were mailed to the insurance companies for payment. The transitions in dentistry have been many, and, while I wasn't there for the switch from stand-up dentistry to sit-down dentistry, I experienced many revolutionary improvements. Digital radiographs and online patient records minimized the need for cabinet space but increased the need for technological training. Team building was another aspect that required enormous effort. Having spent my own early working life on road crews, in copper mines, and construction crews, I had a personal awareness of life as an employee and wanted to make sure that I wasn't seen as "one of those bosses." Together we had regular Team meetings, retreats, continuing education trips, and, as a result, I knew that my practice had, in many ways, become my new training center. It was so much more for me than just a place to fix teeth or a place to work. The best part for me was seeing the children and dealing with the parents as the following chapters will explain in greater detail. Had I known in 1973, when I was on the brink of quitting dentistry, what I know now, there's no question that I would do it again, possibly better, but not likely with more enjoyment. Even against some odds, including a 21% rate on my start-up loan, it was one of my best decisions.

SECTION THREE- KIDS SAY THE DARNEDEST THINGS

You only treat children?

People are often confused or surprised by my choice of specialty. It might be due to their own history in a dental chair or their vision of how difficult it must be providing dental care for children. I have imagined that the picture in their minds must be one of wrestling alligators in piranha infested waters. I must admit, I am amused by all of this, since the reality couldn't be further from the cartoon-like ideas that inhabit peoples' minds. In the generic sense, let's look at some of the reasons why I enjoy treating children.

1. They are honest

2. They are funny

3. They don't use drugs

4. They are smaller than I am

5. They are not as smart as I am

6. They don't smoke

7. They are suggestible

8. They are not biased against dentistry

9. They are curious

10. They are capable of learning new skills

Those are only the first ten that come to mind immediately. I'm certain there are many more reasons, but that short list should provide some idea of how and why children are so profoundly different than adults. I admire them in many ways, but I know I did not "learn everything I know from children." They are cute in many ways, challenging in others, and the rewards of helping them navigate a potentially difficult situation are enormous.

In this section I want to share some of my stories about how children have endeared themselves to me through their curiosity, humor, honesty, and generosity. While I cannot recall every single moment in my career that touched me, some remain so vivid in my mind that I can experience my emotions all over again while recalling them. In fact, two of the stories, when I tell them to an audience at a dental conference, nearly bring me to a standstill as I try to control my own feelings. It is a part of the legacy of my career those precious times when some unexpected words reached out and went straight to my heart, sometimes amusing me, sometimes melting me, and always leaving me with the satisfaction of knowing that my life and that of my patients were very much intertwined.

NOTES:
It's possible my teen-aged patient might have used drugs, but I never sensed that in my practice
Some children are biased because they learned it from their parents

CHAPTER 1

I have a trick

Taylor's Trick

Entering the new patient room is always an adventure. A name and age appear on the schedule, but little else. Occasionally there is a history from a referring dentist, but typically the little one waiting in the room would be a mystery to me. The first-time ever visit is a crucial step in gaining the trust of a child, and I was always sure to enter slowly, introduce myself and begin a light, but important conversation. It was also a time that I would begin my evaluation of the child in terms of age-appropriateness, social ability, and focus. I often thought if I had three new patients all at one time in a single room, it might have made a good circus. The children would be all over the place in terms of behavior and activity. Some would nearly recoil in anxiety and others would be very much up front and engage me before I had a chance to say a word. No matter what the interaction, this moment was key in establishing a relationship of trust.

A well-known mantra of the business world is "time is money." In terms of productivity, I can not only appreciate that, but understand it on many levels. My experience in pediatric dentistry has always been that time is far more than just money. It is an investment. The moments I spent with a child would ultimately pay back greatly. There was never a question about the reality that with a healthy and trusting relationship, productivity would be higher. But in a deeper sense, those initial connections would become the seed from which a much greater reality would develop. By taking just a few moments to concentrate on the child rather than the teeth, something special would result. One of the first articles I published in a dental journal was entitled, "Are You Treating the Tooth or the Patient?" The genesis of this idea was from one of my patients in dental school, who provided me with one of the most profound and useful insights I could have ever learned.

The filling appointments in dental school were scheduled for three hours. Did it really take that long to fill a tooth? No, but each and every step of the procedure needed to be checked and approved by an instructor so that a student couldn't run wild without guidance. The result of this reasonable concept was that patients paid almost nothing for the dental care they received, but they also had to endure appointments that included separate "checks" from instructors for each the following:

1.   Cavity check (to make sure there really existed a cavity on the targeted tooth)

2. Local anesthesia check (to allow the student to obtain the necessary Novocain)

3. Rubber dam check (required of all filling appointments in dental school)

4. Decay removal check (to make certain all the decayed areas had been cleaned well)

5. Prep check (the final 'drilling' on the tooth must conform to a specific shape and size so that the "prep," or *tooth preparation*, had to be approved prior to filling the tooth)

6. Matrix band check (for proper placement of materials to help shape the filling)

7. Filling check (to see that the filling was shaped and smoothed sufficiently)

Because the clinic floor often had forty or more dental students with three or four instructors, it was not always immediate that each of these checks could be done. At times there were delays before moving on to the next step. I am convinced that every person I ever treated during my days in dental school was guaranteed a spot in heaven for their patience during this process.

A quick aside about dental terminology. In the American tooth numbering system, which is *not* universal, the permanent teeth are counted starting from the upper right had wisdom tooth, which is labeled tooth #1. The next tooth forward, the twelve-year molar, is tooth #2 and so it proceeds around the dental arch until one reaches the left side wisdom tooth, which is tooth #16. Dropping down to the lower dental arch, the left wisdom tooth is #17 and so it continues to the right-side wisdom tooth, which is tooth #32. With this simple convention, dentists and their staff members can efficiently talk about a given tooth with a universal number rather than the more cumbersome, "lower right second bicuspid," which is conveniently #29.

Having explained that, I had a young adult male patient in my chair one day and I was treating his upper right second bicuspid tooth. Each of the afore-mentioned steps were done in order and, at the end of his appointment, I removed the rubber dam, thus giving him the first opportunity to talk in nearly three hours. When I asked him how he was doing, he looked at me and asked, "Are you open to feedback?" Feedback is a way of life in dental school and is often not always positive, but I realized that he had something he wanted to say. I told him that I would be happy to hear his thoughts. What he said was simply, "My name is Rick." I responded and told him that I already knew that. He looked at me again, and this time emphasized one word by saying to me, "my NAME is Rick." Perplexed, I asked him what he was trying to say to me. What followed was so clear and so important that I still recall the moment nearly fifty years later. He said, "Each time you called the instructor over, you said to him, 'would you please check #4.'" Stunned, I realized he was correct. So preoccupied with the tooth I was treating, I had forgotten that it was attached to a living, breathing human being, and, that person's name was Rick. Hence, my published article about treating the tooth or the person.

Back to the new patient room. We often had six to eight new patients each day, so I had much experience with meeting children for a first time, but some remain embedded in my memory. One of those was when four-year-old Taylor was waiting for me and the moment I stepped into the room, he burst out, "Hi Dr. Psaltis. I have a trick." Rarely did a child give me such a gaping opening to begin a dialog, but Taylor launched one of my favorite back-and-forth exchanges. When I asked him what trick he had, Taylor quickly said that he could stick out his tongue and touch his nose. This was hardly new territory for me, but I responded with amazement, and before I could even finish telling him how impressed I was, he asked if I wanted to see his trick. Playing him a bit, I said that his mother had brought him in so I could count his teeth. His eyes grew big, and he said that he really wanted to show me his trick. When informed that we may not have enough time for that, the boy then grew more animated and nearly begged to show me. I turned to his mother, who was seated in the room, and asked her if it would be all right for her son to show me his trick. She gave the go-ahead and without hesitation, Taylor stuck out his tongue much like a snake and tapped the tip of his nose. I acted duly enthused and told him that I had a trick, too. "What's your trick?" Taylor demanded. "I can stick out my tongue and touch my ear," I said. Eyes wide, the boy insisted that such a thing couldn't be done and asked me to show him my trick. I said that we had used up a lot of time with his trick, so that I needed to move on to looking at his teeth. He returned to the pleading role, and I again asked his mother for permission to take a moment to show Taylor my trick. She agreed. With that, I stuck out my tongue and, with my index finger, touched my ear. "THAT'S NOT IT," the boy said. When I reiterated that I had done exactly what I said I was going to do and repeated the "trick," Taylor began to laugh out loud. I had spent about one minute in this entire sequence and now had the boy on in the palm of my hand. The relationship was born, and the time it took was only momentary. Did this time create more money for me? No. But it certainly created a relationship.

On another day, three-and-a-half-year-old Zach was waiting for me in the new patient room and when I entered, he looked at me, did a double-take, and then began to stare at me with a surprisingly penetrating look for such a young child. I engaged Zach in the usual ways, but not without being distracted by his unending stare. The dialogue:

Me: "How old are you, Zach?"
Zach: "Three and a half years old."
Me: "Have you been to a dentist before?"
Zach: "Yes."
Me: "How was that experience for you?"
Zach: "Good."

At no time did he stop his fierce concentration on my face. It is always unnerving when someone looks at me with such intensity. Did I have some breakfast on my lip? Did a pimple suddenly emerge on my face? Was my nose running? Why was Zach staring?

Me: "Zach, are you looking at something?"
Zach: "Yes."
Me: "What is it that you are looking at?"
Zach: "Your glasses. They are the coolest glasses I have ever seen,"

Me (now relieved): "Thank you, Zach, but it looks like you don't need glasses."
Zach: "No, but if I ever do, I want glasses that are just like yours."
Me: "Wow, Zach, how do you think you'd look in glasses like mine."

At that point, he raised his two hands, make circles with his fingers and placed his fantasy glasses over his two eyes.

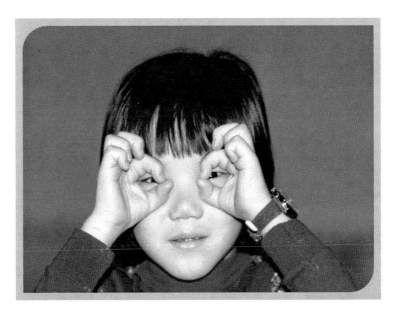

Zach demonstrating "my glasses" on his face

Once again, how much time did I spend on this child? It may have been a minute or two, but however much time I took to find out what had fascinated him, it created a connection that made the initial examination easier and more fun. While it didn't work every time, it never took much to bond with some of the children who were open to connecting with me. I always hoped it was as much fun for them as it was for me.

Years after Taylor's initial exam when he had reached high school, he would saunter into my office in the way that only a teenager could, and, with a big smile on his face, greet me with the phrase, "I have a trick" and then stick out his tongue and touch his ear with his finger. We'd both laugh, and then have an easy and comfortable checkup for him.

CHAPTER 2

My art gallery from patients

My mother was an artist. So was my older brother and so is my older son. I never was an artist, but I can appreciate the talent required to produce wonderful art. My preference is toward impressionists, which may account for why I was always appreciative of the artwork that came into my office. Some of the children clearly had some help from their parents, and others, equally clearly, did the pieces entirely on their own. If the medium is truly the message, each one showed me that my patients understood our connection in ways that they felt must be shown in a picture or a message. How could I not be touched by them?

I treated each item given to me as though it were a masterpiece. Honestly, some of them were pages of coloring books that looked as though they had been colored by a blind person. However, I never forgot that, for that child, in that moment, it was a gift to me. The "quality" or accuracy of the picture never meant as much to me as the mere fact that children brought something intended for me. I was their dentist. I took no pictures to Dr. Wainwright.

My acumen as an art critic would never result in a job at MOMA or any other gallery, but the examples included here are some of my favorites for varying reasons. Carly was a delightful eight-year-old girl when she came into my office with a radiant face that simply exuded excitement. Subtlety has never been the strong suit of children, and, when they walked in with a smile as wide as the room and a paper in tow, I knew I was in for something special.

Carly had been a patient for three or so years and was one of those children who talked to me rather than shying away. In spite of her age, she was engaging, friendly, and simply a very nice child. When she handed me the above picture, it was a fair depiction of her lying on the dental bench, but the message she wrote was what pulled at my heart. "Thank you for being a community helper" were her words. I could only hope that she was referring to the care I had given to her, but I was moved enough to fail to ask. A child reached out to me.

Olympia is located at the southern-most tip of Puget Sound and, as a result of that quirk of geography, the area from which my patients came was quite large. For most of my years in practice, the next pediatric dentist west of me was in Honolulu, the nearest pediatric dentist east of me was on the other side of the Cascade mountains, and the closest one south of me was in Vancouver, Washington, which is across the Columbia River from Portland, Oregon. As a result, some patients literally came from three hours away for their dental care in my office. Sad to say, I failed to write the child's name on the back of following picture, so I cannot credit him/her for this piece of artistry.

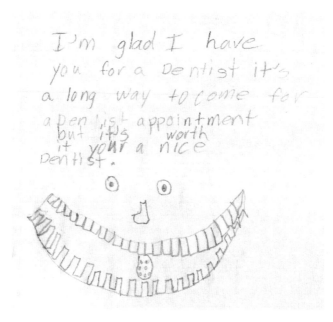

While it is cute that the child drew fifty teeth into the enormous smile, it is the message that struck me the most. Not knowing the artist, I cannot say the distance the child came, but apparently it was a "long way." The idea that this youngster would take the time to draw this self-portrait (or so I assume) and tell me that I was a "nice dentist" hit its mark. I always appreciated that children are honest. Sometimes they are brutally honest, but I admire that. When I got a compliment of this sort, it meant a lot to me and inspired me to continue the style of care that I had set as my goal and my philosophy. It seemed that the children understood.

Amy was one of the most consistent artists to share her talents with me. Always engaging, she would come in with her father, who was likewise friendly, positive, and wore a happy face. I appreciated them both and accepted Amy's efforts with much enthusiasm. This particular piece of work was an actual card that she'd made and is not to scale. I was happy to give Amy plenty of slack for her spelling since she was still so young.

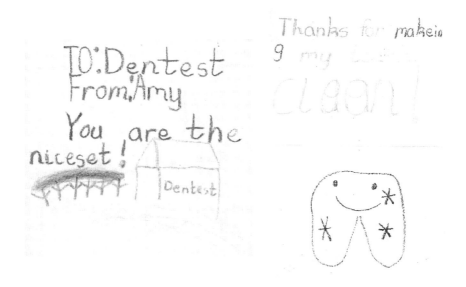

She missed her description of my job. I understood that she was telling me that I was "the nicest" but I had to wonder if I was actually the "nice set." I opted for the former. The inside of her card also reminded me of how easy it was as a young child to not plan the spacing correctly when creating a written document. Unlike today, when our word processors correct spelling, grammar, and shift words onto the next line, it may be easy to forget that at one time, any letter than didn't fit across the width of the paper could be bumped into the next line, just as the "g" in "makeing" remained detached from the word. Thanks, Amy. You were also the niceset!

Like Amy, Michael made me a card. It had a nice fold in it and was innovative in that by folding the inside in half, the cover, shown below on the left, completely covered the entirety of the inner page. This card, too, is not shown to scale. I can't recall if Michael brought me this during the holiday season, but judging by the hat on the tooth, it might seem that Christmas was in the air. His depiction of a molar was remarkably accurate, and the fact that the tooth was holding not only a toothbrush, but also floss, put Michael near the top of my preventive dentistry students. I imagine that adults who have experienced tooth pain may well opt to express gratitude to their dentists, but children are more prone to head to the prize basket at the end of an appointment. Michael apparently understood I had cared for a tooth that must have hurt him and he took the time to make a card to tell me "Thanks for fixing my tooth." I appreciated that, but I also noticed the closing of his note. "Your friend, Michael." I have said that people wonder why I treat children.

A picture (and the signature, in this case) are worth more than a thousand words, and they serve as a part of my reply.

While I often noted the occupations of the parents of my patients, I didn't know them all. I did get some clues, however when some of the notes from the children were handed to me. In the case of Ashley, who was a kindergarten student, my strong suspicion was that she probably wasn't a talented typist. Perhaps her mother was a secretary, but more likely she was a supportive mother who wanted to assist her daughter in expressing her feelings.

Gregory L. Psaltis, D.D.S. P.S.
222 Lilly Rd. N. E.
Olympia, WA 98506

Dear Dr. Psaltis:

I like to come to your dentist office because you are nice to
people and gentle and you take care of my teeth. I think your
helpers are nice to me because one time when I was there I
was crying and they wiped my tears.

Sincerely,

Ashley

Once again it was the sentiment related that made this nicely typed note
so special. I shared Ashley's words with my Team members because they
were the "helpers" who wiped away her tears. These words impacted me
in numerous ways. Realizing that my co-workers were also motivated to
help our patients be comfortable and cared for could not have made me
prouder. When one works with like-minded people, anything is possible
and, that was a part of the "magic" in the practice. Even Ashley knew that.

Gratitude is one of the gifts I received in many forms. Adults can express
it verbally, but children were not always quite as eloquent. Their gratitude
came out in slightly less direct ways, but often in the form of the cards and
pictures they created for me. They helped me be more gracious in accepting compliments. For a long time I would deflect them, claiming that my
team members were mostly responsible for a child's good experience. The
simple cards and pictures had an economy of words with a treasure trove
of meaning.

None of these pieces of art will hang on the walls of billionaires or be auc-
tioned at Sotheby's. They will not be stolen in the middle of the night by
art thieves and won't appear at the Uffizi Gallery in Florence, Italy. They
are, however, precious to me for reasons I trust the reader will understand.
They have lived with me for as many as forty years and they come out of my

file with some frequency. Thank you, children, including those whose pictures aren't included here, for making my work meaningful and emotional. I wish I were the artist that all of you are.

CHAPTER 3

Call 'em like you see 'em

Dental hygienists are often criticized for preaching too much, spending too much time scraping away at the dental buildup that their patients failed to prevent, or hurting people while doing their job. I can understand all of that, although I don't agree. Dentistry is an interesting profession in that we do our utmost to coach people into not needing our services. When people refuse or forget to do the minimum homecare that has been recommended, the onus of treatment invariably falls on the dental provider. Hygienists are a talented group of professionals who do what others will not—clean teeth thoroughly. It's unfortunate that people tend to consider them in negative terms. I certainly don't. In my home state of Washington, the laws allow trained dental hygienists not only to do all the traditional things that everyone knows, but they can also do injections and place restorations. This is not a universally popular concept, as some dentists feel that only a person with a DDS or DMD degree can do these procedures. While there are techniques that are extremely complex and require significant training and skills, much of the work of dentistry is digging a hole and filling it up again. This is not to minimize the importance of doing these procedures well, but for the basic "restorative care" (filling teeth), an advanced degree is not really necessary. It is a mechanical skill that can be learned and performed by dedicated professionals, which dental hygienists tend to be. When I have discussed this idea with my fellow dentists, I occasionally get a glare that indicates their opposition to the possibility that someone other than the king or queen of the practice could be up to the task. My experience with several hygienists taught me they most definitely can do the work. After all, since the fillings they place are checked by the dentist, is it reasonable to think that they would accomplish anything less than excellent care?

Another thing I find attractive about dental hygienists, particularly the female ones, is that they are typically very professional in their demeanor, dress, and communication. It could be the extra two years of training, their good income, or simply a natural selection process, but whatever it may be, they usually present a very good image. As a male, I do not write this as a sexist commentary, but rather as a compliment to their status as health care professionals. I appreciate this aspect because if a hygienist is working in my practice, she is a representative of my office, and I want people to notice the care that she takes to keep herself healthy, fit, clean, and attractive in dress. (Note: I have never had a male hygienist work in my practice, although the hygienist in my own dentist's practice is male, and he, too, projects a positive image). I have never interviewed a hygienist on this topic, but I like to think that all of this is the result of their own pride in themselves, a characteristic that I admire.

Having said all that, I must now relate that some of the most challenging parents in my practice are hygienists. It's not likely what you might expect. They do not want to check their own children's teeth after we have cleaned them, and they don't want to do the injections on their own children. It has nothing to do with any of the procedures. In their neat and tidy world, there is no room for dental decay. After all, they provide the ultimate in preventive dental care and no child of theirs should ever have a cavity. Unfortunately, their children *do* sometimes have cavities, just like every other child on the planet. I have always felt that when a dental hygienist receives her RDH (Registered Dental Hygienist) degree, she might feel that her entire family will now be immune from tooth decay. It is not easy to explain that their children do not arrive on the earth with an inborn skill of brushing and flossing, nor do they have a revulsion of candy and sugar.

Children of hygienists, just like children of dentists, including my own, are not "dental people." They are just regular kids and do all the things regular kids do. They might be a bit sneakier about stashing their Halloween candy in a secret spot, but they do have it.

Austin was referred into my practice because he was a management problem. He did not want to cooperate with the family dentist, and he had some fillings to be done, so he came into my practice. His mother, a very personable individual, happened to be a dental hygienist, and she could not believe that Austin had cavities. She was also embarrassed that he was so resistant. From my perspective, not every child is angelic in the dental chair, so I don't judge the child or the parent when I have one who doesn't want to be a willing partner in the process. In many cases I can talk to the child, encouraging him/her to understand what is being done and recognize that it is not as difficult as they might think. Austin was buying none of it. While not my favorite way to treat children, I felt he would need a mild sedative to keep him safe while I was using my high-speed equipment in his mouth. His mother sat by, anxiously watching, and expressing gratitude for my patience with her son. All in a day's work. When we finished his treatment plan, she told me that she wanted Austin to be a regular patient in my practice since her dentist did not seem to be able or want to deal with Austin's behavior. "That's fine," I told her, "and I'll see you both again in six months."

It is often the case that once a child has been treated, she/he will return to the practice six months later, six months older and six months wiser. That was the exact situation with Austin. He confidently strolled into the office, lay on the dental chair and my assistant gave him a dental cleaning without a peep or resistance from the boy. He was now about seven years old and his mother, now the proud parent of an ideal patient, sat nearby witnessing the magical change that had happened to her son. As is the case with all the children who come in for a check-up, I only see them after the cleaning has been completed, so that in my own world, all children have clean teeth! As I walked up to Austin, he was lying down on the dental bench and glanced up backwards to see my approach. "Good morning, Austin," I said to him. That was greeted by his face gnarled into a confused expression. He looked up at me once, then again and finally blurted, "Who are you?" When patients have been sedated it's not uncommon for them to have amnesia and besides, it had been a half-year since the boy had seen me anyway. "I'm Dr. Psaltis, Austin," I replied, then added "I'm the dentist who fixed your sugar bugs when you came here before." Austin again looked at me, twisted around on the chair to get a right-side up view and after a moment or two said in a voice loud enough to be heard in the entire treatment area, "Oh. I guess I haven't seen you since you shaved your head."

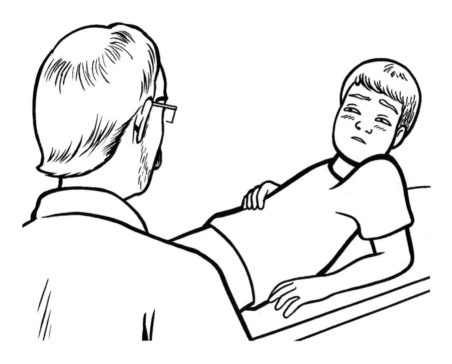

There was a momentary pause in the room. It was the proverbial pregnant moment when the next thing to be done was unknown. Austin's mother, who now wore a shocked expression on her face, knew exactly what she had to do. "Oh, my goodness, Dr. Psaltis, I am SO sorry for what Austin said," she said as her own face reddened. I began to laugh out loud because the boy's comment was so nakedly frank. He reported on what he thought he saw. Too young to be vicious, Austin may have never seen a bald man in his young life and possibly couldn't figure out how my head had come to be covered with skin only. For me it was a ripe moment of child humor, but for Austin's mom, it was a horrifying moment of her son making a public faux pas that was inexcusable. Among my many thoughts in the moment was that I rarely saw a dental hygienist appear so utterly lacking in composure. I was also reminded of the occasional agony of being a parent. As far as I was concerned, Austin simply called it like he saw it.

CHAPTER 4

What's in a name?

For ease of pronunciation and spelling, I have occasionally wondered how much simpler my life might have been if my last name had been Smith, Brown, or Jackson. None of those names cause any difficulties. With the mysterious silent P at the beginning of my name, many people are already stumped. Because I always wanted my patients to call me Dr. Psaltis rather than Dr. Greg, it posed some rather amusing variations from my patients that still tickle me to this day.

Having lived with my last name for 73 years, I have come to appreciate it in many ways I might not have expected. My grandparents immigrated from Greece, and, unlike some Greeks, whose names are multi-syllabic, they never changed theirs. It is the original. The anglicizing of first names was common to fit into the American culture more comfortably, such as my father's name, Gus. Greek tradition is very clear—the first son is named after the father's father, the first daughter after the father's mother, etc, and so it was for my dad. His grandfather was Kosta, a nice Hellenic, but not overly strange, shortening of the full name of Kostantinos. Some of those Kostantinos became Dino while others took on the more phonetic homonym of the shortened Greek name, Kosta, which became Gus. My father never really liked his name and always told my brothers and me never to name a child after him. So much for tradition.

However, when it came to Psaltis, he was 100% tradition. While I have learned to live with the idea of spelling out my last name every single time someone asks for it, it remains a bit cumbersome to repeat over and over, "Yes, that's Psaltis, spelled P as in Peter, S as in Samuel" and then proceed with the rest of the letters. The variations over the years have amused and amazed me, including Spaltis, Paltis, Baltis, Lapitis, Palitis, and my favorite, Splatis. It is not unusual for people to ask how my name is pronounced and depending on my mood, I will tell them it is pronounced "Saltis" without the P, much like psychology or, when I'm feeling more playful, I will tell them it is the same P as in psychotic. As a cultural tidbit, I am always happy to inform them that in virtually every other language the P is, in fact, pronounced. When the reply is something to the effect that it would be so difficult to pronounce the PS sound, I merely ask a simple question—when you go to a second floor on something other than an elevator or escalator, how do you do it? The answer would always be, "I go up steps." "Correct," I would say, "and you just said a ps at the end of that word."

My last name, in Greek, begins with the letter that we pronounce "sigh," but in fact is that pitchfork shaped letter, psi, pronounced in Greek as "psee." It is fortunate for me that I get to separate the letter into two parts for one reason only—the psi in the Greek alphabet is the second-to-last letter. That would mean often being at the tail end of many lists. It's a rather lovely shaped letter and always makes me think of images of Poseidon, the Greek god of the ocean, who is typically depicted with a spear or harpoon with a psi-shaped tip. While all of this may seem confusing to some, it becomes easier when I explain that Psaltis is actually a trade name, much like carpenter, smith, cooper, and the many others that are reflective of what an individual did for a living. To further clarify, I say that it comes from the same root as the words psalm and psalter and immediately people seem more at ease, since these are familiar terms with that unusual p in front. The Psaltis of the Greek church is the cantor. He is the one who chants and intones in the background during Greek orthodox services and when I learned this, I found myself more than interested. My grandfather was a stonecutter, so I suppose if he had been such several generations earlier, my name might have been Cutter, Stone, or Carver.

I celebrate the order of the universe when I connected the dots with this realization that my name was of a church official and that as I write this, I hold the position in my own church (not the Greek orthodox church) of Platform Assistant. That, in my church, is the person who backs up the minister with opening the service, greeting people, making announcements, calling for the tithes and introducing any guests we may have. Fortunately, my responsibilities do not include chanting or intoning. While my career has been spent working in the oral cavity of many children, the work necessary to make what comes out of my mouth in a musical fashion would require more years than dental school. I am happy to merely speak with no music attached.

Back to tradition, though. As I mentioned, my father, while not traditional about the rules of naming children, particularly about his own name, was adamant about our family name. I once made the mistake of asking him why we didn't just drop the "P" and make things simpler. My father had a bearing that was intimidating just from his mere presence, so discipline was not often needed for us. When I posed my question, it was one of those times when I saw the anger well up in him. This was not at all expected. I thought it was a good idea, but from the look on his face and the tone of his voice, it was obvious I had asked for the unspeakable. I always admired his ethics—he often told us that the one thing he would not tolerate was to smear the family name. It dawned on me that changing it to what I considered an easier form was among those smears. I never brought it up again.

In their own way, children have a wonderful imagination about words. I like that they can simply come up with a version of a word that is close enough to be recognizable while being amusing at the same time. The little "slips" they occasionally blurt out, such an embarrassment for their parents, but so funny for everyone else, tickled me as well. It has been so with my patients' versions of my name. No parent ever felt shy about sharing those names that their children had dubbed for me. Perhaps it is because my name is already unusual enough that the variations were merely another manifestation of a name that wasn't like Smith or Jones. I long ago decided that the mispronunciations and misspellings of my name were there for my amusement. I'm not sure my father would have felt the same, but I am not quite as traditional as he was. Of all the variations, two that stand out over my years with children were passed on to me from their parents, and two others came in written form from the children themselves.

I had a delightful family with two boys that came in on a regular basis for their checkups and treatment. The boys were quite talkative and engaged me in conversation each time they appeared. Somehow that never failed to touch me that these young people, who only saw me twice each year (or perhaps three times if they needed a filling) would tell me about their school or about something that had happened in their lives. One of them, in particular, would be nothing short of chatty, even at the young age of four or five. I can assure you that I was not in that category with Dr. Wainwright in Elmhurst, so that added to my wonderment. At the end of one of the boys' appointments, the mother, during the consultation, smiled broadly and told me she just "had to tell me something" the boys had said. Of course, I was always curious for feedback, and she told me that before coming in for the day's appointment, Luke, the chatty one, had told her that he "really liked Dr. Sawdust." I laughed out loud and still get a chuckle when I'm working in my woodshop and see the sawdust fly. I think of Luke and just smile.

During my career I also received some funny pictures from my young patients who were doing their best to convey their appreciation of my

work. With all the difficulty of a name like mine, they were not always perfectly accurate, but no less appreciated. Five- year-old girl Amy, who was
in chapter two of this section, brought with her this greeting that included
one of the variations I had never before seen.

Amy was a sweet child who was very cooperative and always smiling. Since
I often found that adults would struggle with my name, it was no wonder
that Amy had her own version. I did wonder if the fact that I filled some
of her teeth might have resulted in Dr. Philtist. She did get the P right,
though, which was no small feat. Of course, it took a small correction to get
past the initial S, which can be seen clearly on the card.

Another child, a little girl named Emily, was similarly friendly at her visits,
and when her name popped up on my schedule, I knew I was in for a treat.
Little did I know the importance she had given me with my name. Once
again, it was during the consultation that her mother told me that Emily
just loved her visits at the office and that she thought "Dr. Solstice was very
special." Twice each year I think back on Emily with fondness.

Steve was the younger of two boys and his mother worked in my office. I
sometimes wondered if she put Steve up to this, but, having known him
for some years, I really doubted that it was anything other than his genuine sentiments. Always with a smile on his face, Steve greeted me at each
appointment while his older brother, also a nice boy, would more likely
stay quiet.

Yet another way to spell my name clearly appears on this picture and I can only hope that the two t's in the middle were pronounced with that sharp sound that is normally spoken. Should they have been softened to sound more like a "d" I'm not sure the sentiment of this sweet picture would have been the same!

All of my patients eventually graduate out of my practice, but Luke, Amy, Emily and Steve, with their variations on Dr. Psaltis, remain with me to this day.

Did I mention that I am not so traditional? Yes, I did. When my wife and I had our son, we considered many names for him and allowed our other two children to join in the fun of potential names. In the end, we named him Kosta. Not Gus, but Kosta. Was it for his grandfather, my dad? Perhaps so. In spite of any problems with the P in Psaltis or the fact that my dad never liked the Americanization of his traditional name, I was drawn to Kosta because it is ethnic without being too strange. I am proud of my Greek heritage, but not enough to name my son something like Agamemnon. What's in a name? Tradition and, in the case of some of my patients, some humor and fond memories.

CHAPTER 5

You can't judge a book by its cover

While I held my own opinions about clothing and makeup styles, I never felt it was mine to editorialize about how my patients came into my practice. The range of clothing (from chic to basic) was broad, and the styles changed with the times. I did my best to be aware of the dynamics of children growing up in spite of having left that situation myself so many years before. Some of the children would come in as if dressed for a formal meal while others literally looked as if they were coming straight from the playground. Since my focus was on their teeth (which also had quite a range of appearances) I felt that any commentary about attire was simply not my job. I, myself, had worn bell-bottom pants, paisley shirts and for quite a while wore my shorts at mid-thigh until I was called on it by a person quite a bit younger than I. We all have our own ways and am as respectful of others' tastes as I can be.

One boy in the practice, Eric, had been a patient since he was a very young child and, when he was about twelve or thirteen years of age, he came into the practice entirely dressed in black—shoes, socks, pants, turtleneck, plus hair and makeup that were clearly out of the gothic style book. Still a good kid, Eric became utterly mute during his visits, failing to say hello, good-bye or anything in between. I never changed my own routines, always engaging my patients in conversation, no matter how superficial or light it might be. To me, it was always about connecting, even when my efforts yielded no responses. Since I had patients with autism and developmental problems, Eric was not the first patient to refuse engagement with me. He was a patient in the practice through all his high school years.

Early in my practice I was introduced to a fabulous book that can be given as a gift at any major life event, including a wedding, a first child or a graduation, among many others. The Dr. Seuss book, <u>Oh, The Places You'll Go</u>, became one of my office's traditions in that we would give a copy to the patients who stayed with us until they graduated from high school. Each Spring we would order several copies and would write a note of congratulations into the inside cover of each one. From the time there was more than one dentist in the practice, we would each sign the books so that all of them were ready to present at the end of the appointment that most closely aligned with the graduation. It was a heartfelt note that reflected our pride in the accomplishment, and I must admit that I often wondered if the recipients felt as strongly about their own success as we did. No matter, we gave the book regardless of the reaction of our patient.

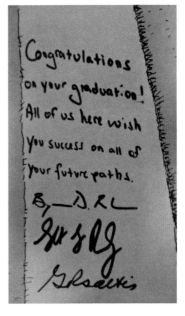

The cover of the Dr. Seuss book...   ...and our note of congratulations

Everyone in the practice was aware of Eric's transformation and unwilling-ness to speak with us. Among ourselves, we would lovingly refer to him as "Mr. Gothic," as he was the sole representative of that genre among our clientele. However, we were respectful of him each time he came in for his appointment. Frankly we appreciated that it is occasionally an actual gift to not hear anything from a teenager! We all went through it, the traumas, the changes, and we somehow survived. It's difficult enough to transition from child to adult without any added stresses, so we mindfully kept his nickname to ourselves.

Each morning we would meet at 7:15 for a huddle to discuss the day's schedule, including who was coming in, when we might need more sup-port for a fearful child, which parents wanted to be seen "absolutely on time" and which ones were talkative. We would also remind ourselves of any problems or difficulties that had arisen at a prior appointment to make sure we could acknowledge them during the current visit and make sure the children and their parents were aware that we were on our toes.

One Spring morning, one of the assistants, during her review of her patients for the day, mentioned that Mr. Gothic was about to graduate from high school and asked if we would be giving him a book. The question surprised me a bit because I saw no reason to deprive Eric of our acknowledgment of his achievement. "Of course we are," I responded while wondering what sort of reception we might get. Since we hadn't heard a word from him in several years, it was difficult to imagine if he would be grateful, use the book as a frisbee and throw it across the room, or what. I confess that I was slightly apprehensive, but steadfast in my commitment to all graduates.

The practice always scheduled our high school patients in the afternoon since we felt they were the students who really needed to be the classroom. Somehow a second grader missing an hour of class didn't feel quite a signif-icant as a student who was in a higher-level class. Eric's appointment was at 3:30, our last check-up time of the day. As he had for years, he entered the office in his usual clothing and again failed to utter a word. He lay on the bench, and I greeted him and lightly chatted during his exam. He had always had a healthy mouth, so when I had completed my examination, I gave him what had become his standard report. "Well, Eric," I started, "you have no cavities today and everything seems to be very clean in your mouth. We'll put the fluoride on your teeth, but I'd like you wait a moment before leaving." He looked at me wordlessly, and my assistant proceeded with the fluoride application. I walked into my private office, pulled one of the copies of Oh, The Places You'll Go off the shelf and wrote the date and the personal salutation to him. I then returned to the operatory, which is the room where all the treatment was done. In a pediatric dental office, it is common to have an "open bay," meaning that the chairs are not separated by walls. In this way the patients don't feel so isolated, plus the entire team can observe all the patients at one time. Many questioned the wisdom of this and asked what happened to the patients when a child started crying. This is a question that would only be asked by someone not in the specialty. My experience taught me that when any child walked into the open bay operatory and saw the other patients sitting quietly, it was reassuring to her/him and typically resulted in a better outcome.

Because the open bay concept entails inclusion of several dental chairs in a single room, the level of activity is normally intense, with patients, assistants, hygienists, parents, and doctors. There is cleaning of teeth, using suction to clear saliva, and the noise of the air-driven hand pieces to provide the treatment. On the day of Eric's appointment, I walked out of my private office into the operatory and instantly noticed that it was deathly quiet. No doubt all the team members had the same question hovering in their minds that I did about what would happen next. As I approached Eric, he was now upright in the chair so that I could engage him face-to-face as opposed to the more typical dentist-over-patient position. My traditional presentation was always similar to this: "Eric, I understand you are graduating from high school and all of us here are proud of you. I hope you are proud of yourself. We have a gift for you as a way to express our congratulations to you on your accomplishment." At this point, I would hold up the book for the patient to see, making it clear that I was about to give a Dr. Seuss book to an eighteen-year-old. "We have written a short note to you inside the cover," I would continue, "and hope that you will enjoy this book that we feel is very appropriate to the occasion." Next, I handed the book to Eric with my left hand and extended my right hand to shake his. Eric paused a moment, then took the book, but only looked at my hand. He did not shake it. What happened next was both unexpected and profoundly educational. Eric opened the book and silently read the inscription, apparently taking his time to read the short message carefully. When he closed the cover, he stood up, stuck out his hand to shake mine and, in a rather loud, but sincere voice, said, "Thank you very much. I've always felt like I have been treated well here." With that, he walked out with the book. It is an understatement to say that we were all stunned. The first thing we heard from Eric in several years was a heartfelt statement of thanks for the book and it reminded me that in so many ways, you can't judge a book by its cover. The same can be said of a person.

If this story ended right there, it would already be rich enough. The story, however, does not end there. One year later when my older son was off for his first year of college, he invited me to come up to see the campus. I may have been the person who invited myself, but either way, I went to Bellingham, Washington, to tour the campus of Western Washington University. My son took me to his classrooms, the gym where he worked out, the art studio where he studied in his major, the food halls and, naturally, his dormitory. I enjoyed the entire tour but was reminded about the amusing fact that if you take the letters in the word "dormitory" and rearrange them, it will spell "dirty room." That, in my mind, is poetry. The grand finale of the tour was to the bookstore where the family tradition would be fulfilled of buying a coffee mug from the college our children attended. As I looked around at the textbooks, computers, sweatshirts and other paraphernalia, a voice rang out across the expansive room, "Dr. Psaltis!" When I turned in the direction of the shout, I saw Eric approaching me with a broad smile on his face. He was no longer Mr. Gothic. His clothing had changed, as had his hair and other makeup. Desperate to recall his actual name, the best I could do was to stay quiet and greet him visually and with a hearty handshake. "What are you doing here, Dr. Psaltis?" Eric asked me. I explained that my son was a freshman and was showing me around the campus. For lack of anything meatier to say, I told Eric that "I didn't know you had come to Western Washington." He said that he loved it there and, when my son returned to my side, Eric introduced himself, took out a piece of paper and a pen, and began to scribble away. When he was finished, he handed the paper to my son and said, "This is my dorm room number, my email address and my cell number. If you need any help with anything, just get in touch with me. Your dad is the greatest dentist."

As I have always maintained, pediatric dentistry is about the relationship. I have no way of knowing how Eric's choice to go gothic was received at his home, but I can only surmise that being treated in the practice in the usual, respectful way, must have affected him. I don't know of any patients who ever judged me for the quality of the fillings I provided. The magic comes from something else. As with all parents, I was so grateful that another human being had reached out to care for my son. That could have been how many parents in my practice felt. Much like Dr. Seuss's book, it's what inside that counts more than the cover.

CHAPTER 6

You are/were my dentist

Are you a teacher?

Not every child who left my practice made me sad. Some practically made my day when I discovered they were going elsewhere. For the majority, though, it was hard to realize that these young adults had matured beyond the walls painted with gnomes, wizards and other characters that were intended for younger children. It is the ultimate fate of most of the patients in a pediatric practice to transfer into the dental office of their parents. To be quite honest, I would most likely have been lost with the procedures they might require when they were older. My last adult patient was my wife and if she needed a filling, I'd refer her out of the practice. Permanent teeth were never my thing and apparently permanent patients weren't either. As I have related, some were more difficult than others to lose. Saying good-bye to some of them was as emotional a moment as I can imagine. I felt they were lost forever, but that proved to not be true.

I was recently in my bank to conduct some business, and I posed a question to one of the bankers. She told me that she would need to call in Alicia, the branch manager, since she would know the answer to my question. As I waited, I heard footsteps coming down the hall and Miranda asked me if I had ever met Alicia. In spite of the mask on her face (due to the COVID situation) I could see the smile on her face and the twinkle in her eye. "Oh yes," said Alicia, "Dr. Psaltis treated my teeth when I was a child." We reminisced for a moment before getting down to the business at hand, but I reveled in the thought that here was a woman who would choose to bring that memory up. My memories of my childhood dentist in Elmhurst, Illinois, were not ones that I would happily bring up if they didn't somehow shed a light on my own personal dental history. I was also reminded that another of the employees in the bank had been a patient of mine as well.

I am an espresso junkie. I own a Swiss-made espresso machine and enjoy my coffee each morning. However, prior to my retirement, I was only home in the morning and my desires for a great cup of coffee would arise again during lunch time. I was a brown-bag lunch guy. I would pack my sandwich, my fruit, and head off to the office knowing that even if my morning ran late, I wouldn't need to rush off to a fast-food place to grab anything I could find. My lunch awaited me in the fridge. It was the espresso that would occasionally draw me out of the building during my break time. Olympia, like most towns in the 21st century, is blessed with many coffee shops. I always went to the place that made the best drink. Once, I ordered a dry cappuccino and waited patiently until the order was ready. The barista was scooping the foam into my cup with an earnest look on her face. It held her focus so much that she first saw me when she offered the cup for me to take. As she did, she hesitated for a moment, squinted her eyes, wrinkled her eyebrows, and stared at me for a moment. Finally, she blurted out, "Are you a teacher?" When I told her I was a pediatric dentist, her face exploded into a grin and she said, "Dr. Psaltis, you were my dentist." While I have a remarkably good memory for names, especially the names of my patients, I could not recall this young woman in spite of her name tag. In fairness, many of my patients left the practice when they were still children, not young adults, so to place a name on a face that had changed over the years was a challenge. It thrilled me (and them) when I succeeded, especially if I could remember the names of their siblings. Alas, that didn't happen for my barista, but I still appreciated the fact that she would appear so happy about seeing and acknowledging me.

My younger son became entirely enamored of the Tour de France when he was in middle school. The private school he attended required an eighth-grade project for all the students who would be graduating. It was impressive to see what these talented young people would devise. I often felt it was the middle school equivalent of a dissertation for a PhD. Some wrote plays, some painted, some built computers from scratch. With my son's enthusiasm for the world of bike racing, he decided his project would be entitled "Becoming the next Lance Armstrong." Because the history of the individual has now unfolded, this subject may not strike the reader as a particularly good choice, but one must recall that prior to the exposés about his misdoings, Armstrong was nearly a god-like figure. Not only his biking prowess, but also the story of surviving cancer and becoming a champion. So, my son, Kosta, began a nearly Herculean regimen of working out. He would pedal away from our home and not return for an hour or so. My wife and I laughed at the fact that he would bike much farther than we would allow him to drive a car. It didn't take long for him to become a serious competitor and once he met a local bicycle coach, he joined the Rad Racers Bike team. His principal skill was in Cycle Cross, a sport that combined mountain biking with steeplechase. Much like the mail, neither rain nor snow would cancel the races and we could go to cheer him on, bundled up like Arctic explorers. At one point, he had risen up to a national level ranking. As his competitiveness and discipline mounted, he determined that his goal was to win the Tour de France. Not satisfied with such a lofty goal, he further stated that he would take French in high school so that he could deliver his victory speech in the language of the host country. Never one to discourage my children, I supported his vision. When Kosta began classes at the local high school I asked him how he liked his classes and teachers. He would talk about his biology teacher, who had also been a favorite of Erica and Reid, my other two children, when they attended North Thurston High School. He would also mention his algebra instructor, but, as he worked his way through his daily schedule, he paused for a moment and said he really liked his French teacher. He told me that she had told him that he had a very good French accent and that, oh, by the way, I was her dentist when she was a girl. She had taken her husband's last name, so it provided no clue, but on parent-teacher conference night I made a point of visiting the classroom. When she told me her birth name, I could immediately recall her sister's name as well. As described above, it was a fine moment for both of us. Kosta, by the way, decided to not make cycling his lifetime work. Once he went to college, his biking days became only for fun.

Another common occurrence was to encounter an existing patient. It seemed that it was most often a younger child and happened in grocery stores. I'm sure there were other places that I met the children in the practice, but it mostly seemed to be there. I might be walking down an aisle in search of something when suddenly I would feel arms wrapped around my legs. Looking down, I rarely came up with the child's name instantly, so I would provide a smile and a generic question such as, "Have you been brushing your teeth?" Since I didn't have a lot of friends who were three-four-five years of age, I figured it was a safe bet that a child hugging my legs was a patient. The parents' response was a nearly universal apology for their children hugging me. From an Emily Post standpoint, I can understand that sentiment, but from a humanistic point of view, I marveled at how a child would come right up to her/his dentist and greet me. For me, it was a mark of success in that I felt the child had seen past the physical part of an appointment and seen the personal. I wore these encounters as a badge of success with my patients and always told the parents so. Typically, they would respond with some positive remark, which enhanced my sense of doing dentistry in a fashion that was different than what I had experienced.

If I were to recount every instance like this, it might overwhelm the book. Suffice it to say that since I retired, I have encountered many of my former patients, proving that they hadn't entirely left my life but rather had taken on a new role. It's not lost on me that there may be other former patients who see me and, for whatever reason, choose not to engage. Knowing that must be true, I can only hope that it wasn't because of some form of trauma I had inflicted on them. I never tire of hearing someone tell me, "You were my dentist." The phrase itself connotes that for children, I was truly *their* dentist. I was not the mother's dentist, and I was not the father's dentist. I was *their* dentist and that was special enough that they still talk about it.

CHAPTER 7

Decoding foreign terms

I was never a car guy. When friends who are "car guys" talk to me about their "hemi V-8" I can only wonder if it is a knockoff of a vegetable juice I drank as a child. I have learned a few things about cars, such as solenoid, camshaft, and other labels on car parts that are pieces of the engine, but I really couldn't begin to identify them, replace them, or do anything with them other than say I am familiar with their names. If I had really wanted to know all of this, I would have gone to auto mechanic school or bought a "Car Engines for Dummies" book, but I am happy knowing that other people have done that, and I pay them to handle my car's parts. That's lucky for me.

Dentistry is much the same. I have always understood that before I went to dental school, I could not explain simple things like an MO on tooth #3 (tooth one-six in other countries). I don't expect non-dental trained people to understand it either. This is largely why I have always used terminology that children can understand. However, when a child is in the dental chair in my office, I communicate in the most efficient manner with my team members, which might include a phrase such as "MO on #3." This phrase, to most people, is as foreign as Άνοιξε το στόμα σου, Καλαμαράκια or POTZEP. Fair enough. Using this "foreign language" has brought unexpected humor and enjoyment to a workday. So it was with Josiah. I could identify with his errant interpretation of my dental terms because I have experienced similar moments when I have spoken in something other than English.

Since I happen to enjoy foreign languages, I have had my own experiences with some odd misunderstandings with people when I have merely tried to have a friendly conversation with them. I learned German in high school and college and now have friends in Vienna, Salzburg and Innsbruck, Austria. I also have two "exchange daughters" from Germany. Each spent an entire year with my family while they were in high school and have now become just like family members. My wife and I head to Austria every other year to visit all our friends. For me, it is my big opportunity to knock rust off my German and enjoy what I consider the magic of saying words that were never a part of my upbringing. They would have been nonsense syllables to my ears as a child, yet they are now meaningful. The challenge of assembling a cogent sentence or even a lengthy story add to my personal enjoyment. In spite of my belief that I can roll German off my tongue with very few technical or vocabulary errors, I have stubbed my toe more than once. Perhaps the classic example of this was when my wife, younger son, and I spent five months in Salzburg as a cultural family experience. While there, friends from Vienna planned to come to visit, and fortunately we had adequate space to house them in our rental unit. We had rented a lovely chalet on the outskirts of Salzburg. It belonged to a couple who lived on the first floor while we occupied the second floor. It had two bedrooms and one "extra" room that could be used as a living room or a guest room. Elsa and her son, Bernelle, would be with us for a weekend and our plan was to have Bernelle stay in our son's room and Elsa would be in the extra room. One problem was that the extra room did not have an actual mattress, but rather a sofa that was not designed to be a bed. I wanted Elsa to know this, so I wrote her an email to explain the situation. Because of my confidence in my German, I failed to verify the word that I was certain was the one for "mattress." When I wrote to Elsa that there was plenty of room in our rental unit, but unfortunately there was no "Matrose" for her, it must have tickled her. To my eye and my ear (and apparently my brain) the word looked like, somewhat sounded like and, therefore, must be the one for mattress. After sending the email I decided to double check my note and discovered that "Matrose" actually means "sailor." I wasn't sure if Elsa thought I was trying to set her up, but failed, but she took it all in good humor.

I also practice my Spanish by doing my best to write to my dentist friend, Doctora Valeria, in Zihuatanejo. We have both laughed at our language gaffes more than once. Until I learned how to add a tilde above a Spanish "n" on my computer, I would simply write the word without consideration to how it changed the meaning. Valeria pointed out to me one time that I had written her a note expressing my enthusiasm for returning to work with her in the following year. When I wrote it, the Spanish word for year, año, takes on a considerably different meaning when the tilde it not there. It is the word for the opposite end of the alimentary tract from where I typically do my work. No doubt Valeria understood what I meant but must have smiled when she read it. She, on the other hand, had told me about having a visitor in Zihuatanejo and, during a tour of the area, the individual pointed out that there had been a tremendous amount of construction since his last visit. "Yes," Valeria told him, "There are many new condoms here now." This, of course, was while she was pointing at some new high-rises going up.

I literally learned my primitive Greek from a book. Compared to my abilities in German and Spanish, I can hardly say that I am even casually acquainted with the language. My brain was always in full gear, trying desperately to understand my Greek relatives who wanted to share conversations with me. I would listen, pick out the four words (out of twenty) in a sentence that I felt I could grasp, and then fill in the rest of the sentence with my best guess as to its meaning. One of the times I was in Athens, I took a woman to visit my relatives because I thought she would enjoy seeing a Greek home and meeting these wonderful people. Most of the time was spent in awkward silence, but occasionally, a sentence would come out—either from me after arduous efforts to assemble something that made sense, or from them at a pace that all but insured I would quickly be lost. My uncle was looking at me and my friend, whom I had dated and to whom I was still emotionally tied, and he spoke to me with an eager expression on his face. The words I heard were "when, you and her." I was fairly certain I had also picked up "see," so I invented the sentence, "When will you see her again?" Pleased with myself, I felt I could answer the question because I had understood it. "This summer," I told him. To that, there was great joy and big smiles from my relatives, all of which told me I had not, in fact, understood the question. Out came the Greek-English dictionary and I discovered that he had asked me when we would be married. While I know it is better to say nothing when an undecipherable question is posed, my enthusiasm often overtakes my good sense.

The language of dentistry is like any other foreign language. Without training, it is not easy to know what is being said by a dentist any more than I can translate hemi overhead V-8, or whatever it is that big, oily, powerful cars and trucks possess. I prided myself on always being able to make my treatment recommendations clear not only to the children with the specialized vocabulary, but also to the parents. An example might be a procedure called a pulpotomy, which is a cousin to a root canal, but only in that there is a nerve treatment involved on the primary tooth. In fact, the roots are not even a part of the procedure. To that end, I always called them "nerve treatments" so that the parents could possibly grasp what I was recommending for their children. There were also abbreviations for most procedures so that the members of the dental team could easily and quickly relate. An example of this would be that we routinely placed a stainless-steel crown on a badly decayed or broken-down primary tooth. This we called an "SSC" for obvious reasons.

The new patient room was often the scene of many dramas. I never knew what to expect, either from the child or the parent, when I entered the room. As a result, I needed to be fully present so that I could size up the situation as quickly and effectively as possible. This was based purely on the outward appearances of the occupants. At times the parents were sitting back on the chair with their arms crossed and a scowl on their faces, and other times they would smile, stand, and extend a hand to shake mine. The children also varied from being utterly mute, if not outwardly fearful, to being like Josiah, my eight-year-old new patient on that particular day. My second foot had not even made it into the room before Josiah, whose feet were enthusiastically swinging back and forth off the edge of the bench, began his high-speed soliloquy. Without ever taking a breath that I could notice, Josiah proceeded to tell me his story. "Hi, Dr. Psaltis. We have a new dog at home. His name is Blackie because his fur is all black. We used to have another dog, Spot. Spot was a good dog, but he got hit by a car and he's dead now. We got Blackie to take his place. He is great. He has a long tongue, and he wags his tail all the time. He's so friendly! He licks my face when I get near him, and I like to pet him. We also have a cat named Fluffy. She got that name because her fur is really fluffy. I like her, too, but she doesn't lick my face and she doesn't like being petted. She also jumps on my lap and sometimes her claws dig right into my legs and it hurts." Unlike this written version, there were no periods I could discern in his story. Josiah rolled all this information out without a pause. I was mesmerized. How he got so many words out of a single inhalation remains one of the astonishing moments of my career. As Josiah was spinning his story, I looked over at his mother, who had that "here we go again" look on her face. Finally, I stopped the boy and told him we needed to count his teeth, but that we could talk about his pets again after I was done. "Can we?" he asked with his big eyes staring at me and his feet still looking like a pair of pendula.

Much to my surprise, Josiah lay back in the chair without saying another word and opened his mouth wide for me to peer into it. As was sometimes the case, I was looking into a severely compromised mouth with multiple teeth that would require both a pulpotomy and a stainless-steel crown. The convention we had adopted in the practice was to dictate the treatment plan one tooth at a time so that my dental assistant had time to enter the information into the patient's chart. The medicine I used at that time for the pulpotomy procedure was called ferric sulfate, so that our shorthand for the task was FSP. One final note about tooth nomenclature. In the United States, primary teeth are labeled with letters starting on the upper right, coursing across to the upper left, then dropping down to the lower left and proceeding to the lower right. Different systems exist in other countries, but in the USA, the upper primary teeth were A to J and the lower primary teeth were K to T. Now that you are educated in the terminology that we dental professionals share, let us return to Josiah and his exam. It always breaks my heart to see a child who will be facing extensive treatment. Somehow in the case of this boy, who had instantly captured my heart by impressively pouring out his detailed stories about his animals, it was even more difficult to realize what lay ahead for him. Little did I know what lay ahead for me. Keeping all the terminology in mind, here was what I dictated to my dental assistant:

A= FSP, SSC (I hope you now know his primary upper molar needed a pulpotomy and crown)

B= FSP, SSC

C=SSC

H= SSC

I= FSP, SSC

J= FSP, SSC

With each statement, Josiah's eyes grew bigger and bigger and the fact that he was not able to continue his conversation with me must have also gnawed at him. It was hard to know which played a bigger factor, but I sensed that if I proceeded directly to his lower dental arch, he might explode. So, I stopped for a moment and asked him the question I occasionally asked other patients who appeared to be totally attentive. "Do you know what I'm talking about, Josiah?" I asked the boy.

Without hesitation, Josiah looked me in the eyes and said, "Yes, Dr. Psaltis. I've been listening the whole time and I think you're talking about Mississippi."

It was at that moment that I flashed back on Elsa, Valeria and my Greek relatives and their response to my unexpectedly humorous gaffes. I normally can maintain my composure while at work, regardless of the situation. I call that "being professional," or in other words, I don't say what I'm thinking. In this case, I could only let out a hearty laugh and tell Josiah that he made a very good guess, but it wasn't Mississippi. From there, we started talking about his animals before I got back to his lower primary teeth which led me to another tour of Mississippi.

Chapter 8

Thanks

Most patients who were referred into the practice were management problems of one sort or the other. It was sometimes the actual care they needed, meaning procedures that family dentists didn't do often enough to master. More commonly, it was the behavior of a child who was simply unwilling or unable to cooperate. I didn't try to figure out why this was the case, but rather focused my attention on how to reach the child verbally, create a different relationship, and move ahead. There were other factors that were also important in establishing a new perspective beyond the terminology, such as the décor of the office.

My first office had a wall-to-wall rainbow that included colored venetian blinds that were placed in such a way to match the painted walls and create a continuous arc of colors. Birds floated above from the ceiling and the chairs, which I built myself, were plywood boxes with an upholstered top. While this verbal description may not sound overly attractive, they were both esthetic and practical in many ways. Built to the exact height I wanted children to be situated, the chairs required no adjustments, no electronics, and had no moving parts. When parents first saw them, they often considered the beds to be shaped like an ironing board or surfboard. All of this was by intention in order, among other things, to have the environment look very different than any previous dental office the children may have visited. It also wasn't lost on me that to construct each chair cost about $150 in wood, stains, Naugahyde and foam (plus my own labor), as opposed to the more traditional dental chair that cost about $3500 each. When I opened my practice, saving that kind of money before the first patient had walked through the door was one way to keep the loan amount down while still having an appropriate piece of furniture.

I knew other pediatric dentists who went further than I was willing—some constructed their offices as if it were a train station, and the dentist would wear clothing similar to an engineer. Another had cartoons on the walls and put whiskers on his mask to make him look very much like a mouse. I was never big on dressing up and felt a need to maintain a semblance of professionalism (as I defined it) and wanted to be known as Dr. Psaltis. My upbringing did not include the concept of calling any adult by the first name. It was always Mrs. Johnson or Mr. Nelson, but never Julie or Mark. Besides, other than some stereotypical movies, I had never heard anyone called Mr. Tom or Mrs. Ruth, so the fact that some pediatric dentists wanted to be called "Dr. First Name" never appealed to me. Perhaps it was simply familiarity or a more personal approach, but I do not have many children in my close circle of friends. There was a separation that I felt was important so that I could be the *dentist* rather than the *friend* of my patients. Interestingly, the children ultimately came to see me as a friend in their own way, so the labeling didn't seem important.

The terminology we used was also age appropriate. (See Appendix A) Much like studying the ABCs in elementary school, as opposed to discussions of Nietzsche, it was vital to communicate in a language that the patients could understand and not go over their heads. As with all professions, it would be easy to use technical terms and confuse a child or parent. It was also possible to use some popular dental terms, such as needle, shot, drill, etc., but those terms would not lead to a successful experience. Instead, I would blow sugar bugs with my whistle, much to the amusement of some parents. It was, however, very understandable for a child. In short, the entire office was geared for my clientele: it looked different and sounded different. I approached things differently and, therefore, had different results than those in the offices of the dentists from which my referrals came.

One day a referral came in for a patient whose mother I had met in a different venue. Ross had proven to be too much for the family dentist who happily asked his mom to take him to see Dr. Psaltis. Since I already knew the mother, I was pleased to see her son on the schedule, which remained true right up until I entered the new patient room. There was Ross, at that time a boy of about six years of age, writhing on the dental bed with my courageous dental assistant doing her best to keep him there. Siegfried and Roy might have had better luck. I greeted his mom briefly and got right down to the business of establishing my all-important relationship so that I could move things ahead. Ever the optimist, I opened with my usual questions of how old he was and what grade he was in school. Ross displayed no desire to play my game. He was neither the first nor the last to begin his time in my practice this way, so it didn't really bother me too much. With my assistant holding his hands so that I could focus on his mouth, I completed my examination of Ross and, like the family dentist, found that he was in need of some fillings. My strategy was to use a mild sedative for the child because of his physical resistance. When a child was verbally resistant, such as screaming or ignoring all conversations, I never felt a need to give the child drugs. I was confident enough in my skills to work with them and win them over. Physical resistance, though, created the possibility of danger since a sudden movement at the wrong time could lead to a significant injury from our high-speed equipment.

The sedative was moderately successful, and I completed all the fillings Ross needed in two appointments. It wasn't easy, but the care was good, and his mother was impressed. She also mentioned that she had another son and, for the sake of combining appointments, she asked if she could she bring Scott in without a referral. This is one of the best practice-builders for a pediatric dentist. In the vernacular, I would say, "tame the wild child and capture the siblings." This is a recipe for growth and success. Six months after Ross's filling visits, he returned with his brother Scott, whom I suggested we see first so that he could be a role model for his younger brother. This was a strategy that I commonly used, and, most often, it would work out well. On this day, I would call it a partial success, although Ross was still a handful during his checkup visit. No sedation was necessary, and his mom was grateful that I could complete the appointment.

The boys became regular patients in my practice and with time, Ross joined the legions of excellent patients. He, like many others in my career, was always viewed with the long term in mind. Today's struggles would turn into tomorrow's successes, and I rarely doubted that this formula would fail. One of my pleasures in my career was to watch my patients grow over time and morph from toddlers to little children to big children to teenagers and, in a few cases, to adults. Not many remained in my practice beyond high school, but for those who stayed that long, they had blossomed into young men and women and held actual conversations with me about what they were doing and what their plans were for the future. Watching the maturing process was part of my joy over the years. One of the hardest parts of being a children's dentist is that all of my patients would someday leave the practice. This was, in part, because of convenience, at times because they were leaving for college, and occasionally due to their sense of not being in an environment that matched their advanced level of maturity. I delighted in observing this process, but often was saddened by the loss of another "family member."

Ross and Scott were two patients who stayed with me well into their teen-age years. When I speak of my patients growing, in their cases, it was lit-erally. I don't recall having met their father, but I can guess at his genetics because these two young men both grew to be 6' 6" tall and were two fifths of the starting basketball team at their high school. Standing eight inches shorter than these two, I would smile internally as I looked up at them.... w-a-a-a-y up at them, and admonish them to floss and brush. While the great majority of my time in my practice was far more like running a kin-dergarten or elementary school with the usual diminutive sizes that go with them, Ross and Scott were the outliers, but they remained polite, attentive, and conversant even as they towered over me.

As I recall, Scott left for college, which was often the separation point from my practice and Ross would come in on his own. Far more than on that first-ever visit day, I would be glad to see his name on the schedule. At the end of his appointment, I again told Ross that he had no cavities and that I'd see him in six months. As he stood next to me, I sensed that something was up, and I was correct.

"I kind of hate to tell you, Dr. Psaltis," he began, "but my mom and I decided it's time for me to see our family dentist, so I won't be coming in for any more appointments here." This is never a surprise to me but is sad in cases like his. It was like losing a friend. We both experienced that moment in time when we recognized the mutual loss and stood silent for a short time. Then Ross became serious, looked down at me, and asked, "Do you remember when I first came to see you?" I replied that I did. He then continued, "I was really bad, wasn't I?" "No, Ross," I said, "you weren't bad. You just needed to be in a place where you were comfortable and could cooperate." Already feeling the emotions running through me, Ross hesitated for another moment and turned to me and, with a single word, touched my heart so profoundly that afterwards I needed to go into my private office to regain my composure. He smiled wistfully, stuck out his hand to shake mine, and simply said, "Thanks."

CHAPTER 9

One good deed…

There's the Golden Rule and many other axioms that inspire us to live our lives in the best way possible. For me, I have felt so blessed beyond my expectations that it has not often been a struggle for me to generous. Certainly during the lean days of college, dental school and even in the opening years of my practice in Olympia, it was more difficult to feel abundant. During my years in dental school, I literally counted every penny I spent. Some people say that as a hyperbole, but in my case, I had a sheet of paper to account for every cent that left my pocket. I never felt deprived, nor did I have a latent wish to be wealthy. My generosity during those years was measured in my volunteer service to the children of the mobile dental clinics in California and Greece. For me it was a way that I could give without having to count pennies. At that point of my life, I had more time than money, so giving of my time was the best I could do.

When I opened my practice, the thought of paying off a $100,000 loan at 21%, buying a house and car, plus bringing my first child into existence was intimidating. I was confident, but still had the concerns about enough patients coming into the practice to generate an income that would cover all my expenses. With the encouragement of so many Olympia-area dentists, it was not long before my appointment book began to fill little by little.

The trickle of income turned into a nice flow. I was counting every dollar now instead of cents, but the cost of my life had gone up in a similar fashion. One of the promises I had made to the dentists who said they would support my practice was to accept patients who were on public assistance. In my childhood I had never been subjected to poverty or crippling events that resulted in my parents requesting fiscal help. For that reason alone, the entire concept of public assistance was foreign to me. As a brand-new dentist, I had no idea how the system worked, or the impact on my income, but, since I had told others I would bring those children into my practice, there was simply no question about it.

In brief, the public assistance program for dental care in the state of Washington in the early 1980's was for children. Funding for adults was not available. With this in mind, the greater impact of the system would fall on professionals who treated children. That included me. The reimbursement rate for the procedures I performed was usually in the 30-35% range: if I did a treatment for which my normal fee was $100, the state would pay me $30-35. That was already a challenge but realizing that the average overhead for a dental practice is usually between 50-60% makes it clearer that this is not a profitable way to work. However, the system created still another opportunity for me to donate my time by treating the children.

Eventually I needed to face the fact that even though I was only receiving a portion of my usual fee, dental supply companies did not reduce their costs for materials, and my Team members were still paid at their salaried rate. As a result, I was taking a loss on each child I treated. Not all my patients were on public assistance. The majority of the children in my practice were full paying. As a result, it was still possible to turn a profit, pay my Team, meet my financial obligations, and serve the children who were, in my opinion, less fortunate than I was. Many were wonderful, attentive patients and others returned each six months with new cavities in spite of our best efforts to educate them. It was frustrating at times when I realized that with the treatment being given at no cost to them, the incentive for caring for themselves may have lessened, especially to their parents. There were other factors as well, but having to re-treat the teeth I had already restored nettled me. Some of the children, though, were so wonderful that

I could continue their care without being concerned about the monetary consequences to me.

One hour due west of Olympia is a town called Aberdeen. Because of the geography of the Puget Sound area, I had many patients from the area and among them was a particularly delightful family named the Stevensons. They had two sons, both extremely polite and nice boys. One was outgoing and engaging and the other was more reticent. I enjoyed seeing both of them. They always came with their mother, yet another of the parents who made my day. At some point I was told that they always brought a third child, Doreen, whose mother was somehow compromised. I never learned anything about the health issues of the parents unless they willingly mentioned it. Like Mrs. Stevenson, Doreen's mother was always pleasant and listened carefully to all my recommendations about home care for her daughter. Doreen, because of her family situation, was on public assistance. It just didn't matter to me in her case, as she always came with a smile on her face, clean teeth, and no decay. That could have been my definition of my ideal patient.

I prefer to not get into a lengthy discussion of why I eventually chose to stop seeing children on public assistance. In very short, my schedule continued to stretch farther and farther out as my practice became increasingly popular. There was no question that the failed appointment rate was much higher for the public assistance population than for my paying patients. Suffice it to say, there were also administrative issues with the system, which was my primary reason for my choice to drop out of the program. One of the rules stated that I could not refuse to see any child on public assistance if I was a registered provider. When I thought about a handful of the children like Doreen, it tugged at my heart to think about penalizing her and her mother due to the misbehavior of others and the unyielding system. When I thought the entire issue through, I decided that I would, in fact, abandon the system, but invite several of the children to stay in the practice. These were the ones who showed up on time, took care of their teeth and listened to my professional advice. Doreen was one of them. I sent a letter to every public assistance patient in the practice to inform them that they would need to seek care in an office that was a provider. I also made sure that the ones I wanted to see were told of my decision to have them continue at no cost. I preferred to give my time and expertise to those who wanted and appreciated it. I asked the parents that they not inform their children, so that all of these young patients would continue to feel welcome and that nothing had changed. I also asked that they not publicize my decision. Every parent expressed their gratitude and life went on. As each child reached an age of graduation from the practice, my public assistance population disappeared, and the entire episode was forgotten as a short, but important chapter in the practice. For me, it was an extension of the volunteer work I had done for children.

Several years passed and a letter showed up in my mailbox in April, 2002. The return address was Portland, Oregon. There was the name of a store not of my acquaintance, so I first thought it might be and ad of some sort. Far from it. I opened the envelope, and a lovely, hand-written letter was inside. It was on brown stationery and as I read the words, I felt a swelling inside me. It was from Doreen and contained a message that went straight to my heart. This is what she wrote:

> "Dear Dr. Psaltis,
>
> I surely miss seeing you and thought I'd take the opportunity to tell you so. As a child, I remember swelling with pride when the subject of "dentists" would arise. "My dentist is special; he just works with children!" It was not until I was much older that I learned that your generosity enabled me to continue my visits. This gesture of kindness is very significant to both my mom and myself. When I think back on some of my most treasured memories with the (Stevenson) family, many involved trips to the dentist. We all think so highly of you.... I feel that it's so important to recognize and openly appreciate those in one's life that have made a positive influence. I know that someday your gesture of kindness will inspire a similar one in me. I hope that you and your family are well. I'll keep in touch.

Again, thank you….
(Doreen)

30 April 02

Dear Dr. Psaltis,

I surely miss seeing you and thought I'd take the opportunity to tell you so.

As a child, I remember swelling with pride when the subject of 'dentists' would arise, "my dentist is special, he just works with children!" It was not until I was much older that I learned that your generousity enabled me to continue my visits. This gesture of kindness is very significant to both my mom and myself. →

When I think back on some of my most treasured memories with the family, many involved trips to the dentist. We all think so highly of you…

I feel that it's so important to recognize and openly appreciate those in ones life that have made a positive influence.

I know that someday, your gesture of kindness will inspire a similar one in me.

I hope that you and your family are well. I'll keep in touch.

Again, thank you…

Even though I wondered who broke the news to Doreen, I quickly let the thought go and read the letter a second time. In 155 words, she gave me a gift far superior to the dental visits I was happy to provide for her. I do not extend favors or share my skills or time to get something in return. With her short, sweet, and deeply touching note, Doreen again reminded me that it is impossible to know at a given moment the impact one can make on another's life. For me, she was a nice girl with a nice mother. She had apparently not had the good fortune I had as a child. The simple act I had done, once revealed, must have touched her in the same way that her letter touched me. Is it any wonder that gratitude is dearer to me and appreciated more than dollars? I have no way of knowing how she is doing now, nineteen years after her note. I also do not know how her mother is doing. What I do know is that both are still in my memory and for that, I can only be grateful.

CHAPTER 10

A memorable patient

I prided myself on always treating every patient with the same degree of care and energy. I had days when I, myself, was less energetic and may not have had the same amount of patience as on others. In spite of that, I genuinely felt as though I was successful in giving the children in my practice my best. The range of children was as broad as can be expected. Some were chatterboxes and others never said a word to me. Some children appeared very happy to be at an appointment and others were clearly less enthusiastic. There was the range in ages, as well. Once the standard of care for a first-time dental visit became six months of age, that range stretched from six months to the occasional college student who would stay with me. From my perspective, all of this provided a tremendous variety of experiences so that I never felt that I was in a rut. The procedures that I performed were far more repetitive than the children for whom I did them.

This entire section of my book is dedicated to some of the most unforgettable children I saw during my thirty-six years in private practice. Often amusing and occasionally touching, these people represent some of my fondest memories of being in practice. In many cases, it was something they said or did that sparked that memory, but for a few of my patients, it was simply them and their manner. It wasn't some cute word or sentence they said, but rather it was something much more central to their very being. I looked forward to each of their visits more to catch up on what was happening in their lives than cleaning or filling their teeth. I could easily enumerate several but there was always one who stood out for her many years as my patient.

Elisha was referred into my practice when she was about three years of age because of some treatment needs and because of her reluctance to cooperate with the family dentist. Blond and cute, Elly, as her mother liked to call her, was initially a challenge because of her fears, but we managed to work our way through her appointments and complete the treatment plan without too much trauma to either her or me. At the end of care, her mother, Mrs. Fontaine, asked me a question posed by many other parents of my referral patients. "If Elly goes back to our dentist and has more cavities," she began, "would she be referred back here to have them fixed?" I told her that was likely since the referring dentist would probably have treated her the first time if he had felt he could or wanted to do it. I already knew the next question that Mrs. Fontaine would ask, and I was correct. "Since she was referred into your practice, is it possible for Elly to become a regular patient here?" There were few ways that my practice grew faster than through this sort of situation. A pediatric dental practice is different than every other specialty practice. If a patient was referred to an oral surgeon to have wisdom teeth extracted, that person did not become a regular patient in the oral surgery office. That is also true with orthodontics, endodontics (root canals) or most other specialty practices. Pediatric practices are free-standing for children whose parents opt for a specialty practice much as they might select a pediatrician for their children's medical care rather than having the family doctor see them.

When my speaking career began, I wanted to be able to show my audiences the reality of pediatric care. It was always strange to me that pediatric dentistry was often viewed as the least desirable of all fields in the profession, so I wanted to provide some visual images as well as my enthusiastic words about its wonderment. I hired two professional cinematographers from a local company to come into my practice for two days and "film everything." I did not point to any particular patients but gave them free reign to record whatever they could. I got releases from all parents to allow this to be done. As it turned out, one of those days was Elly's first six-month check-up visit. The recording of that event became a staple of my discussions about how fearful patients return to the practice after having gone through treatment.

Elly, escorted by Carina, one of my most talented dental assistants, walked tentatively into the operatory clutching her bright red Elmo doll. At that time in my practice, every appointment that included a cleaning began with a Polaroid photo. I felt it was a wonderful way to begin with something so familiar and also provided a segue to "taking pictures of your teeth," which was our verbiage for obtaining x-rays. Elly, as the video clearly showed, was still uncertain, but in no way resistant as Carina ushered her over to the flamingo painted on the wall. When asked if she wanted Elmo in the picture, Elly made clear that was not a part of the plan. One of the many aspects of the picture-taking that I always liked was that the majority of the children, including Elly, had been either trained or inculcated into smiling for any picture. This lovely, but dour child suddenly lit up when Carina gave the command and the picture was that of a totally happy, smiling child. From there the video, in its edited form, continues with her cleaning during which she was absolutely cooperative. As I approached Elly to examine her mouth, she opened before I could even ask her to do it, and I knew we had a "converted" patient. She was now entirely on our side. Little did I know how prophetic that thought would prove to be.

Every visit with Elly was better and better and any hesitancy she may have shown on that recording disappeared as she became an ever-increasingly confident patient. She became one of those patients who would report to me what was happening in her life. Her mother, who would usually accompany her to her visits, would likewise talk with me about life, about being a mother, and, of course, about Elly. Within a few visits, it became more like a family visit, which I enjoyed on all levels. As with life, the years seemed to pass quickly and by the time Elly became a young woman, she would always greet me with her fabulous smile and a hug.

At one of Elly's appointments, she came in and presented me with a copy of her senior picture. Hers was not the only one given to me, and each one underscored what I had hoped to create

Elly's senior picture

in the practice—a sense of family. I would not have considered giving Dr. Wainright a copy of my senior picture when I graduated, and the gap between my experiences with him and Elly's experiences in my practice showed me that I had brought a different approach to dentistry. It was with a bit of surprise each time I'd see Elly's name on the schedule after that because I knew she had gone to a college that was an almost five-hour drive to my office. Still, she came in each six months for her checkup with her

smile and her stories. One day I received an announcement of her graduation from college, the only college announcement I ever received in my
years of practice. When I saw her name on the schedule shortly after that, I
knew the inevitable time had arrived to give her the news about her future
in the practice.

Each pediatric dental practice has its own philosophy about how long a
child should and can remain a patient. There is no universal rule about
this. Some only allow patients to stay until the end of eighth grade so that
during high school, the care can be provided by a family dentist. In some
ways this makes sense since my specialty requires that I limit my practice
to children. By the time most teenagers reach high school age, all primary
teeth have been lost and potential "adult" dental problems are more likely
to arise. Also, when the child leaves for college, a relationship with the
family's dentist will have been established so that check-up appointments
might coincide with those of the parents. I never established a firm policy.
I left it up to the patients to make that determination. The variability of the
choices always interested me in that some felt far too "sophisticated" by the
time they were ten while others stayed with me past the time they could
drive themselves to the office. Some of my favorite patients were the ones
I called "boomerang patients" in that they would declare they were ready
to move on to their parents' dental practice. Some returned twelve months
later with an astonished look on their faces and the stunned exclamation,
"Do you know what they do in that place?" Terminology and approach
are everything.

When Elly's name popped up on the next day's schedule, my receptionist
called Elly and told her that I wanted to see her at the last appointment of
the morning and that I was going to take her to lunch. She was the only
patient I ever took to lunch. She came, a college graduate, proud of the
accomplishment and still wearing that same winning smile. We hugged. I
checked her teeth. I told her that it was time for her to move on to a family
practice with my gut twisting inside, knowing that I would miss seeing
her and hearing her news. Then we went to lunch and had a wonderful
conversation that was anything but a dentist-patient exchange. At the end
of the meal, I gave her a good-bye present. I had a copy of the video of her

as a first-time check-up patient and showed it to her. Then I gave it to her. I could only hope that it was as meaningful to her as it was to me. Many patients were memorable, but only one got a lunch and a gift. For me? The gift was having her as a patient.

At her final appointment in my practice

CHAPTER 11

Just unreal

Pediatric dentists are unique in the profession in that they have a free-standing practice to which patients can visit by their own choice (or that of their parents), and also a referral practice for children who, in some fashion, did not get along with the family dentist or vice-versa. The referrals often posed a challenge since they were most often behavior problems. The child didn't want to cooperate, couldn't cooperate or, in some cases, had a significant medical history that resulted in the need for specialty care. Among those patients were children with special needs. My strategy with all children, regardless of the special need, was to speak to them as if they were in every way normal. This I did primarily for myself. I was never the high, squeaky pitched voice person who gushed over children or treated them as if they could only hear words at the falsetto level. I wanted them to be as informed as they could and to that end, I spoke with them in plain English. As previously mentioned, I used specialty terminology, but never with that "seeing a newborn for the first time" voice.

The children with special needs came with many variations within a given spectrum. Among my patients with Down Syndrome, for example, there were high- and-low functioning children, and at times it was hard to imagine that they both had the same syndrome. One of my patients, a child with Down Syndrome, was a moderate-functioning child and I enjoyed seeing him each six months. I did not have lengthy conversations with Gil, but he was always cooperative in the chair, and it was no struggle at all to complete any care that was necessary. Apparently, Gil and his parents also enjoyed seeing me because years went by from his initial examination until he was a fully grown adult and became my first-ever patient with a mustache and beard. He was a good-sized young man, and I was grateful for his demeanor.

On the opposite end of the spectrum was a boy with autism. He was neither verbal nor cooperative and, as he grew bigger and stronger, even his father struggled to manage him. Evan began in my practice as a fairly easy child to examine but a difficult child to provide the cleaning of his teeth. I was never asked, but I wondered if any of my dental assistants would request hazardous duty pay. Evan was physically resistant, and it took two assistants, his father and me to accomplish a routine visit. As he got larger, this process became increasingly difficult and we would see Evan in our quiet room, which was euphemistically named since it was reserved for our patients who were not quiet. Evan and his father entered the room, and my assistant went in to prepare everything for the day's visit. Shortly afterwards, she literally came running out of the room as Evan was now nearly wrestling with his father about sitting on the chair. I went in and immediately recognized that Hulk Hogan might have been useful for the appointment. In the end, the boy did not take a seat and we had to schedule him to be seen under a general anesthetic. By doing so, we could complete all necessary care, including x-rays, and any necessary fillings and sealants. While I never thought of these cases as failures on my part, I always wondered if there had been just one more thing that I could have done to have completed the care with the child awake.

Not all referrals are as dramatic as Gil or Evan. Many are nice children who simply need more support than I suspect some dentists were willing to give. Dentistry is a fee-for-services profession, but the services for which fees can be collected are solely about procedures. There is no fee for being patient with a child, spending more time, or simply being kind. For me, it went with the territory, and I ultimately received far more satisfaction from managing a fearful child than filling a tooth. The challenge was always to find a way to connect with a child. Since some children were non-verbal, there was no specific feedback about what was working and what wasn't. In some ways it was like playing darts in the dark. I knew what it was that I wanted to accomplish, but I couldn't always see how to achieve it. Experience helped. For the most part, my philosophy was to remain calm, quiet, and soft in my approach. At times it required that I became louder or harder, and, with that, I appeared less calm. I always wanted my agitation to be kept internally.

A different category of referral was the child who had medical issues that required multiple visits with physicians at a very early age. Never having been that person, it was difficult for me to imagine how profoundly a history of that kind could affect a child. When I was a young boy, my physician uncle performed a tonsillectomy on me, and what I most remember was all the ice cream I received afterwards. This was hardly the type of situation I'm describing for some of my patients. One of my patients, Michaela, had been born with spina bifida. The daughter of a delightful couple, she was referred to my practice, and it was clear from minute number one that she was not happy about seeing anyone who had a title starting with a "Dr." As I recall, I first saw this girl when she was about five or six years old, and she was a handful. I never felt judgment toward these children because I never walked in their shoes, but my desire to make things better for them was intense. In spite of behavior that could (and did) push my buttons, I wanted to provide a wholly different picture of health care. Michaela was not impressed, and we struggled for quite a while.

With this girl the adage "time heals many wounds" was entirely apt. She eventually became a receptive patient and, as with many of my other regular patients, felt more like a friend. I was glad to see her name on the schedule because I knew that I would get an update on her life. Michaela became a wheelchair athlete and proudly reported to me how things were going both in her athletic life as well as her schooling. I admired her perseverance with all she had to overcome, and yet it never felt to me as though she was bragging or calling herself special. I thought she was special, but if she had any of those thoughts, I never noticed. Her exams were usually done with her seated in her wheelchair, which was a bit challenging for me. Having spent my entire career in "sit-down dentistry" I thought about Dr. Wainright and all the other dentists of yesteryear who corkscrewed over their upright patients. For Michaela, I never really minded. She was one of my favorites.

By the time she was in high school Michaela was clearly maturing into a wonderful young woman. On the one hand, it delighted me to see these former youngsters become adults and, on the other hand, it boded poorly for the likelihood of a long-term, continuing relationship. At the end of one of Michaela's routine checkup visits, I told her how much I enjoyed hearing her stories and that I was again pleased that she had no cavities. She smiled that beautiful smile of hers and when I added that I'd "see her in six months," her smile faded. I knew what was next. She hesitated before beginning what I came to recognize as the good-bye speech. Each time it was hard to hear, although I knew that it was the same as having children of my own. The ultimate goal is to set them free and live their own lives even if it comes at an emotional cost to me. "Well, Dr. Psaltis," Michaela began, "I really like being a patient in your office, but I'm seventeen now and it is a little bit weird to be sitting across from a child who's in preschool. And then there are the wizards and dragons on the walls, and I understand why you do that, but I'm not sure it's appropriate for me anymore." I understood every word she said. I find it more difficult to enjoy myself at Disneyland now, particularly since I don't go with any children. Perhaps I'll enjoy it again when I can experience it through the awe-struck eyes of a grandchild. Michaela ended her pronouncement with the phrase that will forever live in my professional lore. "So, Dr. Psaltis," she continued, "my mom and I have decided that it's time for me to see a real dentist." I have no doubt that Michaela had no derogatory connotation in that phrasing, but it tickled me to think of myself as unreal. I said nothing other than my usual wishes for a wonderful future and all the best.

Michaela wasn't quite ready to leave, though, as she said to me that she had something for me as a good-bye present. She wheeled herself out to the waiting room where her mother was seated, and returned with a long, thin box that she handed to me. "Open it right now. I saw this a while ago and thought of you and decided it would make a great gift," she said enthusiastically. Already touched by this sweet gesture from this wonderful young woman, I tore open the wrapping and found a necktie inside the box. On it were little teeth, tubes of toothpaste, toothbrushes, and dental explorers. "The teeth looked just like baby teeth to me," Michaela explained. Speechless, I smiled and leaned down to give her a hug.

Michaela's gift to me

I now wear that tie each time I present a continuing education lecture about managing the behavior of pediatric patients. I tell this entire story about this wonderful child-became-an- adult, show the above picture, and then wordlessly walk down the center aisle of the lecture hall with my sport coat opened enough so that all can see that I was wearing Michaela's tie. I find that it's necessary to remain wordless because of the emotions that rise inside of me as I recall the entire sequence of events. In the end, I may have been Michaela's unreal dentist, but she, like many of my other patients, was unreal in her own unique and marvelous way.

CHAPTER 12

Extended Family—Part I

Like everyone, I have a family of origin. I also have relatives that are branches of the tree from which I came. These people are my family. The adage says that we don't get to choose these people. They are simply ours because of genetics. Now I have a family of my own with a wife and children. One can say that I *did* choose them, and I have a biologic connection with them. I claim other "families," such as my church members, the men from my college fraternity, and the men with whom I share coffee each Monday morning. Each of these families was created out of intention. It may have been a common spirituality, a shared college experience, or a regular social gathering. We are not biologically connected. Some would refer to these groups as "extended family." I rather like that phrase. During my years in practice, I also considered my employees to be yet another family. We spent more waking hours together than most of us spent with our nuclear family members. This is mostly no surprise to me. The *surprise* for me was that the people, both children and parents, who came into my practice, became still another extended family of sorts.

Riley was the three-year-old sister of a classmate of my elementary school son, and she met me at a school function. As was often the case, when adults begin conversing with each other they might either intentionally or inadvertently forget about the children. When this happened, I would engage the children in conversation. These were never meaty dissertations. However, I felt it was important for the youngsters to know that their presence was still noticed, and that any conversation that went over them or without them was not an indication of any lack of love. I squatted down on my haunches to get at eye level with Riley and asked her the usual questions that one might ask a very young child. "How old are you," I asked, and "What is your favorite thing to do for fun?" Some children would not respond, and I would step away, not wanting to elicit any fear. I am well aware that many parents advise their children "not to talk to any strangers," and I supported that concept. With the parent standing nearby, I never felt that it was inappropriate to engage a child. Riley was a delightfully conversant little girl, and she not only answered my questions, but asked me a couple as well. This always delighted me that a child would have the social grace not only to respond to my questions, but also to engage me. This is especially true when the child is only three years old. Our conversation may have lasted for only a few moments, but when I stood back up again, Riley gave me a hug. She was hugging my knees because that was how tall she was. I simply leaned over and thanked her for the hug and her response, looking up at me, was to say, "I like talking to you."

Riley became a patient in my practice not much later and each time she came into my office, she would give me a hug. Over time as Riley grew, her hugs would ascend to my thigh, my waist and ultimately became more of a hug as one might hug one's own child. For me it was a marker event that tangibly showed the level of trust, care and connection that was possible in an entirely non-romantic setting. The idea of appropriateness wasn't an issue, and these brief moments never took on any sense of impropriety. For me it was a show of the degree of connection between two human beings. It just happened that one of us was the dentist and the other was the patient. How could I ever have expected this? Riley was not the only patient who would give me a hug, nor was she the only one who, several years later, invited me to her wedding. I received five wedding invitations from patients. Hugs and weddings always felt very much like "family." I marveled at the fact that I was their dentist.

I was always happy to see Riley and other children who approached me and gave me hugs. This did include some boys, lest the question arise about the entire discussion being only regarding girls. For me it was that rare moment when contact other than my fingers in a child's mouth could be shared as a mutually satisfying show of caring. The critical difference between one's intention with a word or action and its impact must always be carefully considered. In my life, I have had numerous occasions of hearing something that was hurtful, only to have the speaker reply, "Oh, I didn't mean to hurt you." This is a crucial factor in all interactions between two people. I believe that the interactions initiated by a child never had nefarious intent.

The Hanson family was the largest one in my practice. They were always delightful, well-behaved and on time. I appreciated having them on many levels. Mrs. Hanson was engaging and, with her subtle New Zealand accent, provided a rather enjoyable variation in our conversations. Some of her children came in with cavities nearly every time and others remained decay-free from day number one. There were many factors that made some families special to me. Perhaps in the case of the Hansons, it was the number of children or maybe the mother's accent. Whatever it was, that specialness was underscored when I received an invitation to her daughter's wedding. When I tell this story in my lectures, I always ask my audience if they invited their dentist to their wedding. Not many hands go up.

Everyone wishes that life could be one endless joy-filled experience. Eventually we all learn that is an unrealistic expectation. There are bumps in the road. I was fortunate not to have any major traumas in my childhood. The worst thing that happened to me was getting a B on my report card. I had a friend with polio. This, of course, was before the polio vaccine was developed, and this boy carried his left arm in a sling and was not likely ever to use it. That, in my mind, is a tragedy. In high school I had two classmates die: one due to an auto accident and the other by suicide. Those were tragedies. Something of that magnitude never happened to me. My practice was a wealth of joy. The letters, the pictures, the hugs, the gifts, and the many other pleasures that came from my work filled me. Unfortunately, I also had to discover that I wasn't working in the Garden of Eden. Tragedy happens.

When a child vomited in my lap, I could put on a second pair of pants. When patients graduated from my practice, I could savor the memories of their time in my care. When a parent became upset with my work, I could still speak with him/her. When a theoretically irreplaceable employee retired or gave notice, I could still find a person to fill that gap. All of these situations were transitory. They, too, were not tragedies. When a patient died, it was permanent. It was a tragedy that I felt at a profound level. It was not felt as deeply for me as it was for the parents. In spite of that, I could mourn much more deeply than those parents might have suspected.

The two boys in the previously described Stevenson family were wonderful young men. They were among my patients for whom I would smile when seeing their names on my schedule. The older brother, Regan, was outgoing and engaging and remained one of the patients who continued to see me even after beginning his college career at Washington State University. As he matured, I could see a bright future ahead of him as his smile and manner would be welcomed by any organization. One day my receptionist came into the treatment area and told me she had some news that I might want to hear in my private office. This was ominous, but Raquel had been my receptionist almost since the beginning of my practice, and I always appreciated her tact and judgment. We went into my office where she informed me that a phone call from Mrs. Stevenson had relayed the tragic news that Regan had been killed in a car accident. On the day of his graduation from WSU, he and some of his friends had been driving to Moscow, Idaho, which is just across the state line from Pullman, Washington. While under way, a drunk driver had collided with them head-on. My first thoughts went to Regan's parents. It took a few moments to gather myself, and I then returned to my patients, but it was impossible to be my usual chatty self.

The funeral was one week later. I learned the time and place and drove to the Regan's school to attend the service. The size of the crowd indicated the breadth of connection the family had in their community. It was impressive. Those in attendance were of an unusually broad spectrum of ages. I'm certain many had been high school classmates of Regan's so that the more typical funeral crowd of older people was not apparent. I sat near the back as I heard the accolades given by numerous family members and friends. When the service ended, I approached the Stevensons to express my own grief. Mrs. Stevenson, who always brought the boys, told me that she couldn't believe that I had come. For me, it wasn't surprising at all. I had lost a member of my dental family and wanted to be there, however painful it might have been.

With hugs, weddings, and a funeral, it isn't difficult to understand why I felt that the practice had created still another extended family for me. For the Rileys and boys in my practice, it was a delightful realization that being a dentist, a professional not always characterized as humane and caring, could surpass the fears that were more commonly associated with dentistry. When one considers the nature of dental care, it is understandable that patients feel vulnerable as we literally "get in your face" to make our living. When we can see beyond that degree of touching, perhaps a hug may not seem so foreign. I certainly never saw it that way. Attending weddings and funerals also showed a connection that normally only comes with family. I didn't specifically choose these people to be my family, but they definitely became exactly that.

SECTION FOUR– THE PARENTS

They are not the "problem"

I have written that I would always prefer to care for children than adults. This remained true right up to my retirement. I don't really have anything against adults, but my list of reasons for enjoying children in the previous section explains my predilection for them. Adults have pluses as well. Let me count the ways, as I did for children, that I enjoy parents.

1. They make the appointments

2. They pay the bills

3. They (mostly) bring their children in for their visits

4. They give consent for treatment

5. They are funny in their own ways

When I lecture about managing the behavior of children in the dental setting, I begin by telling my audience that I will discuss managing the behavior of three groups: themselves (dentists, hygienists, assistants), children, and the parents. At that moment, I ask the attendees how many, by a show of hands, believe the biggest problem with a pediatric dental visit is the parent. Typically, 90% or more of the hands will go up. I then ask how many of those in my audience *are* parents. For this I will get a range, but normally about 60-70% would raise their hands. My final question would be, "How many of you parents think you are a problem?" At best, I might get five hands (out of 300-500), but I would invariably get a big laugh. It is nervous laughter, but regardless, a substantial response.

Nobody thinks she/he is a problem, especially when dealing with her/his own child. All bets are off, and opinions are free-flowing and clear. It took me time to realize that parents are not really the "problem" during an appointment with their children. More often, I would perceive a degree of entertainment from them as well as rewards beyond the fee I charged. Parenthood changes all of us. We are never prepared to be a parent, but somehow many of us very much want to be one. I truly believe that most parents who came into my office wanted the best for their children, and, while some were occasionally challenging, I honored that sentiment. I am a parent myself and can appreciate the depth of caring toward one's own child. I profoundly appreciated the positive feedback that I received for the work I considered "just what I do."

Parents presented entirely different skill sets of communication, empathy, and patience. They also provided much for me. In the following vignettes, I will more fully expand on stories that involved parents as a main character. I learned much from them all and was grateful for how they entrusted the care of their children to me. I never took it lightly.

Note: Some patients who remained in the practice past eighteen years of age drove themselves. Those sixteen or seventeen can drive but cannot legally sign their own consent until age eighteen.

CHAPTER 1

As different as can be

The concept of two genders is one of the great things in life. There is a book about men being from the Mars and women being from Venus. I believe there is truth in that. Other differences include clothing, makeup, decision-making, need for information and explanation, emotions, and many other ways that men and women are so uniquely different. In the age of gender equality, one might argue that things have become more similar, or equal, but in my mind, there is still a chasm separating the two groups. I, for one, hope there is never absolute sameness. Equality, yes. Being the same, never. I don't believe it is possible due to……. hmm, I'm not sure. Hormones? Upbringing? Culture? Having dealt with children of American, German, Japanese, Mexican, Greek, Vietnamese, Cambodian, and Korean parents, there is a common thread that runs through the ways of being a mother and the ways of being a father. I am inclined to disbelieve the cultural part. But I really don't know. I decided many years ago to enjoy the differences and do my best to meet the needs of both the women and the men who came in with their children.

Let me begin by quoting Mark Twain. I love the man and his wisdom. One of my favorites is this one: "Generalizations are no damn good. Including this one." Today we live in a world of political correctness and sensitivities about anything that might be considered disrespectful. I support this, but as I discuss my experiences with the parents in my practice, it is based on my years-long observations. Consistency becomes reality when it is relentless. Naturally there are exceptions to every rule. I acknowledge that, but in the end, I developed a good sense of how mothers and fathers "generally" were in my office. I trust the reader will be able to understand that and not take offense as I relate my experiences with parents.

How did mothers and fathers differ?

"Your child has six cavities"

Often a very young child was brought into the office with severe decay. When I tell my friends, who are not dental professionals, that I routinely performed baby tooth root canals and crowns on the teeth of three-year-old children, they are stunned. This entity has been known in pediatric dental circles by several unattractive names. Bottle syndrome, baby bottle tooth rot and other more technical, but no less hideous titles. It is currently called Early Childhood Caries (or ECC) with "caries" being the scientific name for decay. It would not be unusual for a parent to tell me that "her entire family always had soft teeth." This was a common way to try to ascribe the problem to genetics. Unfortunately, only the teeth that were bathing in the bedtime fluid, which may have been milk, apple juice, a soft drink like a cola or other sugar-laden fluids, were the ones affected. The way a child swallows is entirely different than how an adult swallows. A child uses the tongue as a piston to press the mother's nipple or the nipple of a baby bottle to express the milk. To better understand that, the reader may want to press the tongue against the biting edge of the upper front teeth to appreciate this mechanism. When a child consumes a cariogenic liquid (one leading to decay) over a long period of time, such as all night, the upper front teeth are the ones that are affected. The lower front teeth and most of the back teeth are not commonly problematic, thus shooting a hole in the "soft teeth" theory. When I presented a mother with this situation, I tried to educate her as compassionately, but accurately, as possible. It was not unusual for her to have a melt-down. I sometimes wished I'd had a couch so that we could have a therapy session. It moved me greatly that the mother, upon learning that she was somehow involved in getting her child into this predicament, would sometimes weep, sometimes wring her hands, and sometimes try to convince me otherwise. Science is a difficult thing to deny, even though it is becoming easier to do so in our current environment. Decay does not develop in a void. There must be a causative factor for it to occur. The factor is not the mother, per se, but she will more likely take on the pain of realization that her inadvertent attempts to help her child sleep comfortably has given rise to some serious dental problems.

The fathers do not have this problem. I have wondered if having the Y chromosome leads males to think, "Y me?" Guilt is not a part of many men's makeup, based on my observations. The fathers of children in need of care typically want to know two things—how much is it going to cost and how long will it take to fix. Beyond that, the interest level in how the decay occurred, what might have been done to prevent it and whether or not it was genetic rarely comes up. A part of me preferred consulting with fathers because the time needed was simply two numbers—the dollars and the minutes. For mothers, it was a seminar with Kleenex.

"Your child's pacifier may be having a negative effect on the growth of the jawbones"

This topic is arguably controversial, although seeing the changes in contour of a child's mouth after long-term pacifier use has convinced me that the results have led to a distorted bite and a change in the position of the front teeth. Once again, the consultation with a father is rather straight-forward and simple. I needed only mention that the pacifier may be leading to future orthodontic problems. Simply mentioning the "o" word was enough. Some fathers stepped up to their children, pulled the device out of their mouths and said something to the effect of "that's it for the pacifier." The children were not often as enthused about this resolution to the situation. However, the inevitable result was quickly accomplished. I never knew how things went back in the home when this sequence of events was shared.

When the exact same phrase was presented to a mom, I would be brought into an explanation of why the child "needed" the pacifier. I was always curious about this and would ask for more information. More than once, I was told that the child needed it when she was stressed. I am not aware of when a two-year-old might be stressed, so I would again ask for more information. "Well, Dr. Psaltis, she gets stressed when we are putting her to bed, when we read to her, when we are changing her diaper......" and I would envision a child living constantly stressed. It was not easy to ask a mother to cease the habit until I hit upon an idea. "Your daughter is so beautiful," I would say, "do you suppose she'll marry some day?" The mother would smile and reply, "Oh, yes, I certainly hope so." I would then ask her, "Do you expect that she will be at the altar with a pacifier in her mouth?" The ridiculous image of this gave the women no option but to say, "No, of course not." "Great," I would say, "then you are in agreement with me that at some point in time between today and her wedding, your daughter *will* stop using the pacifier. Is that what I'm hearing?" Now pondering the question, the answer would be tentative, but affirmative. "Yes, I suppose so," she would reply. "Excellent," I would continue, "and the best time is today." Whether or not that made the final impact I only occasionally knew, but I had to find a way to get through to the parent that the pacifier was not, in the long run, the best thing for the child.

"But aren't they just baby teeth?"

It was not always easiest to speak with fathers. This question came from both moms and dads and is one of the most misunderstood situations in children's dentistry. A variation on this question, when I recommended a baby tooth root canal and crown, was "Can't we just pull it?" I never minded this question because I felt it was reasonable. A few facts about primary teeth, though, would lead to an educational opportunity depending on who was listening. When a father asked this question, I felt his focus was often on money plus the incorrect belief that baby teeth "just fall out" when a child is six years old. There is truth in that. The average age for the *first* baby teeth to exfoliate is, in fact, six. Other primary teeth last until the age of twelve to fourteen. I would then line out some of the developmental information, such as:

- Until the first permanent molars are functional (usually about age seven for an average child) the primary teeth do *all* the chewing of food. When one considers how big a child is at birth and how big a child is at age six, it becomes easy to appreciate the importance of those "baby teeth" to provide the vital function of chewing. There are no others to do it. The job is all theirs.

- While somewhat controversial, much speech development occurs during the first years of life and the front teeth may play an important role during that time. Many of the sounds that are made in speaking involve the tongue touching teeth and loss of those teeth can potentially create speech difficulties.

- The primary molars (back teeth) are typically lost between the ages of ten and twelve. That means that in addition to the critical role during the first six years of life, those same teeth continue the function that enables the child to have adequate nutrition and grow normally up until the age of twelve. For later developing children, these teeth may last until they reach the age of fourteen or more.

- Very much overlooked is the fact that the baby teeth are space maintainers for the permanent teeth that will replace them. All teeth in all mouths want to drift in a forward direction. What prevents that from occurring is having an intact dental arch. Much like a Roman arch, if a single unit is lost, the integrity of the upper or lower teeth will be lost and back teeth will drift so that crowding and orthodontics is more likely.

I am a man. I like being a man and I marvel at the astonishing commitment women have to their children. Mothers want to be educated and make decisions based on that. I fantasize that I am a very capable father, but when my wife was unable to take our son to the pediatrician, I would return from the visit, and she would ask me what "Dr. DeGriff had said about our boy." My report would sound something like this: "He's fine." Needless to say, my report was sadly inadequate, and I sometimes felt that dads (myself included) just can't take in as much information as the moms would want.

Emotions

Mothers were often quite emotive at the end of dental appointments. I never stopped understanding that each child I saw was the precious being of the parents. Mothers would cry when I restored decayed (and unsightly) front teeth, or they would hug me. They expressed their gratitude and would make it very clear that my efforts to provide care for their children was greatly appreciated. I got notes from them on occasion, telling me about their feelings.

Fathers, on the other hand, were far less likely to express emotions. I will acknowledge a couple of memorable instances when this was not so, but as a rule, they were somewhat distanced during the appointments. It was far less common for them to say very much to me, but I knew that the visit was not a social one for all people, including some mothers. Fathers were far more likely to look at their cell phones while mothers were more likely to make subtle attempts to watch over every detail of what was happening.

When I think about all the ways that mothers and fathers were different, I feel as though I could write an entire book about it. My words here are based on my observations of many years, and I trust they will be seen with a sense of humor as my own musings on human nature.

CHAPTER 2

Very bright or gifted

If I were asked what the only two types of children there are in Olympia, Washington, boys and girls would be the obvious answer. However, that's not it. There is a wonderful life force that has kept our civilization going and that would be called parenthood. Given the common phrase, "nobody prepared us to be parents," it is impressive how so many think they have mastered the task at the moment of a child's birth. The utter thrill, amazement, relief (for the mother), and outpouring of love that bursts forth in that single moment is one of the wonders of the world. It never seems to matter that not every baby is beautiful. We are all programmed to tell the new parents that their child is exactly that. We all want to cuddle them, play goo-goo with them, comment on how tiny their fingers are, and delight in the first smile, regardless of the fact that it was probably a random act by the infant. Parenthood fills us, scares us, sobers us, and has the greatest impact on our lives since our own birth. It is monumental and alters our own perception of reality.

I am a parent. I am unable to be objective about my own children. They are perfect in every way. Just ask me. Naturally this is endemic in many parents on the planet. It never failed to astonish and amuse me that the assessment of many parents in my practice regarding their children's IQs was invariably on the high side. As a matter of fact, I noticed that nearly all the children were either "very bright" or "gifted" according to their parents. It's not surprising that never once did a parent enter my practice and proudly announce that his/her child was ugly and stupid. Of course not. They are ALL beautiful and brilliant. No doubt this observation is preferable to the opposite one, and I have seen children who suffered from their parents' negative comments. Staying reasonable always seemed like the best route to take.

In my practice, we had specific terminology to introduce dental procedures to children and we always asked parents to be supportive of those terms. Looking from a distance, they have a high potential for seeming silly. We don't give "shots," but rather we "put teeth to sleep." We don't "drill" on teeth, but rather we "blow sugar bugs away with our whistles." There is an entire litany of other euphemisms, but experience has shown that use of these familiar and understandable words proves remarkably effective in helping young patients not only to tolerate, but to excel at their dental appointments. Had anyone told me during my studies at Stanford that I would spend my professional life blowing sugar bugs, I may have had the same reaction that some parents had, which was "are you kidding?"

Resistance came in several forms. Some parents stated that they felt the terminology was deceiving. Others opined that their children were "very bright" and needed to know exactly what was being done. I never sensed it would be best to explain to a child that I was going to give them a shot in the mouth, put a clamp on her/his tooth, place a rubber dam for isolation, and then drill on the rotten part of the tooth. Over the years I wondered if this explanation of the procedure would suit the parents:

"Today, Aidan, we will use a 27-gauge aspirating syringe to inject approx-imately 0.9 cc's of 2% xylocaine hydrochloride with 1:100,000 epinephrine for vasoconstriction. We will be penetrating your oral mucosa in the area very close to your pterygomandibular raphé in order to obtain an inferior alveolar nerve block to desensitize your tooth."

In fact, that is the most accurate factual description I can possibly provide to a patient, but it isn't likely to go over well with the very bright Aidan, because he is only three years old. It is both my professional opinion and my years of experience that have taught me that it is far more effective to tell the child that I was about to spray sleepy juice to let his tooth fall asleep. Rarely did a young patient screw up her/his face and knit the eyebrows and question this simple explanation. More typically they held still and let me do what was needed. A favorite story/joke of mine sheds light on *adults'* confusion about this technique.

Three-year-old Nicholas came home from preschool and asked his father, "Daddy, where did I come from?" The father, now fully awakened out of his daydream, considered the question with some trepidation, and began his nervous answer. "Well, Nicholas," he began, "someday you will find that you like girls. Eventually you may even find that you like one well enough to give her a hug." At this point, the father is now hesitant about what to say next, but following a deep gulp of air, he continued, "And when you grow up, you will find a woman who you really love, and you will marry her. When you are married there's a….uh….uh….special way to hug her and sometimes when you hug her that way a baby starts growing in her tummy." Now sweating, the father completes the story. "After about nine months, the baby comes out and that is where you came from." Nicholas, who has remained attentive the entire time, says to his father, "Thanks, daddy, for that story. It was really interesting. I was at preschool today and my friend Eileen asked me where I came from, and I didn't know. I asked her where she came from, and she said 'Cincinnati.'"

Adults do not think like children. Children, regardless of their astonishing brilliance, do not think like adults. It's why we read them books like *Good Night, Moon* instead of *War and Peace*. They prefer things to be simple and understandable, which is the specific goal of the terminology I used for many years. I always did my best to coach the parents to support us by not using all the trigger words associated with bad dental experiences—yank, hurt, drill, shot and others. It amazed me at how difficult this concept was to convey, and, in a few instances, I had to ask the parent to leave my practice because of their insistence on telling their children "what I was actually doing." It was somehow especially rewarding to me when those same parents came back to my office saying that their child "wouldn't cooperate" with the family dentist. Perhaps that was because the children didn't want to get shot or drilled.

In spite of our best efforts to educate the parents about his crucial part of our working strategy, it would still occur that a parent, at the end of a child's appointment, would ask, "Did the shot hurt you?" Apparently, the brilliance of the child was not inherited. Tradition is a powerful force, and the urge to still refer to dental injections as "shots" is a tough one to bury. If a child's parent is a bartender, might "shot" not refer to Jack Daniels? If the child's parent is a photographer, might "shot" not refer to a picture? Not as attractive, though, is that if the child comes from an abusive home environment, might it be that "shot" refers to something the parent threatens to deliver to the child's mouth in the case of misbehaving? The word has many connotations and when applied generically, can be misunderstood so easily. I try to avoid it, deferring to the more descriptive terms of the procedure itself—spraying sleepy juice.

Parents weren't the only culprits, though. We all use terminology in our lives. Advertising agents are the best at it, convincing us to purchase things that are far down on our "need" list. However, it particularly amused me when other dentists would joke with me about this effective behavior management tool. Once in a while at my local dental society meetings, one of my peers would walk up to me with a funny look on his face and ask me ironically, "Hey, Greg, are you still 'blowing sugars bugs with your whistle' each day?" This was accompanied by a soft nudging of my side with his elbow. I would smile and reply, "Yes, I do. All the way to the bank." One might say that I was a smart aleck at times, but more important, I was a smart dentist with children.

Lost on the dentists who simply cannot force "sleepy juice" or "whistle" out of their mouths is the simple fact that they, themselves, use terminology each day to their own benefit. My two favorite examples, both of which I experienced more than once in my years of work, were popular and intentional misuses of words to cover up the real message:

1. I entered my new-patient room to see a 4-year-old boy snarling while he was ripping wallpaper off my walls. He laughed

demonically while I introduced myself. He was barely willing even to sit in my dental chair. I asked the mother, who was present, why Colton had been referred into my practice. She responded, "Well, Dr. Psaltis, Colton went in to see our dentist, Dr. Willington. She is such a wonderful and sensitive person, and we just love her. She saw Colton and realized that he had some cavities and told me that she 'didn't want to traumatize' Colton. She recommended that he come to see you." This was a classic use of terminology.

Dr. Willington was undoubtedly thinking to herself, "This child is a monster, and I don't want <u>him</u> to traumatize <u>me</u>. However, she was smart enough to realize that sort of statement wouldn't sit well with Colton' mother. Instead, she modified the sentence by reversing the subject and object, which had a far different, and much more effective, impact on Colton's mother.

2. Another time I walked into my new-patient room and found a beautifully dressed five-year-old girl sitting with her hands folded in her lap and a smile on her face. I began a nice conversation with her and asked her how old she was, if she'd been

to a dentist before, and how the visit had gone. Each time Julia responded with a short, clear answer that left me wondering why she had been referred into my practice. I asked her mother that exact question and her reply was, "Julia went with me to see Dr. Martinson, a man we have seen for the past twenty years. We think he is a fantastic dentist and we felt he would be wonderful with Julia. However, Dr. Martinson found some 'sugar bugs' (short smile from mom at this point) and told me that he didn't have the 'little tools' to work in her mouth." While there are some dental instruments and pieces of equipment that are made in "child size," the great majority of everything we use is the same as a general dentist would have in his practice. Once again, I imagine Dr. Martinson was reluctant to say, "I really don't like working on children," especially to a parent who has been a longstanding and loyal patient. It just could be easier to say that he doesn't have the proper tiny tools.

Both of these examples happened to me and are superb examples of use of terminology. That is not to say that I use my words to deceive or mislead children. I simply want to support them in an understandable way, and that is how pediatric dental terminology plays a crucial role.

Am I cynical about parents' attitudes about their children's brain power? Not really. I applaud parents' efforts to help their children see themselves in a positive light. Are all of the children really very bright or gifted? Not really. But then I do feel a desire to tip my hat to the imaginative dentists in town who didn't want to traumatize the wild child or didn't have the little tools for a young girl. I would have to say that they, too, are very bright, or even gifted.

CHAPTER 3

I'm not a psychic

My name, with its Greek roots, provides interesting conversations and also some expectations. Whether consciously or not, while at Stanford University, I majored in psychology. My speaking/consulting company that I created is named Psilent Productions, indicating the fact that the sometimes-confusing P at the beginning of my name is actually unspoken. When I went to dental school, I joined a dental fraternity named Psi Omega. One might be led to believe that I could have written the Lennon-McCartney song, "P.S. I love you." It felt as though all things "ps" would automatically be a part of my life. Not so. While I believe I am a fairly good judge of character, I learned in my practice that it is, as they say, very difficult to judge a book by its cover. In short, I learned that I am not a psychic.

While my enjoyment of the children was consistent, the expectations of parents were not. I confess that I measured their unspoken goals of treatment by the outward signs I felt I could interpret. Many parents were obviously fearful for their children, which I always considered normal. However, their anxieties would often bleed over into the child's psyche (there's that "ps" again) and the result would be that the child would have the experience at my office that the parent had expected. Children are, after all, very good at reading their parents' signals. They are much better at it than I am. While we coached parents carefully with guidelines for their own behavior, some would either ignore them, not understand them, or simply take matters into their own hands. This was unfortunate. Parents often feel that their children are exceptional.

When I tell parents not to prepare their children for the dental appointment, some would tell me that they always prepare the child, so she knows what to expect. At that point, I would ask the parent, "And how do you prepare your child for a visit to the zoo?" This typically elicited a quizzical stare, but nothing stated. I would continue. "Since you want to prepare Molly for her trip to the zoo," I would begin, "I imagine you would tell her something like this: Today, Molly, we are going to the zoo. At the zoo we will see wild animals that we cannot keep at our own home. That's because some of them, like lions and tigers, have very large teeth and if they lived in our house, they might kill you. Don't worry, though, Molly, because at the zoo they are in cages, so we are safe. However, a few years ago at the zoo in San Francisco, they did have a problem with one tiger cage but only one person was killed." At this, the parent usually laughed and told me, "No, that's not what I would say." When I responded with the obvious question, they would say, "I just tell her that we are going to the zoo." Yes. Perfect. Same with dental appointments. Keep it very simple and do not promise them anything.

Situations of this sort led me to a major change in my treatment philosophy. When in my residency, the topic of parents' presence in the treatment area was a simple one to master. Here's how it went: NEVER! The concept was similar to not letting the fox into the hen house. It will only cause problems, so don't do it. For the first two or three years of my practice, parents were required to sit in the waiting room while their children were having treatment. I had bought into the stories of parents being a problem by blurting out the wrong phrase at the wrong time and disrupting the appointment. The classic would be a parent saying to a child, "They are almost done now, Sheila." This statement came when we were still applying the topical anesthetic and had several more steps to finish the visit. The other factor that led to my change of heart was that I ultimately came to understand that I was, in fact, a poor psychic. Confident that I could determine the goals of a parent, I learned the hard way that I was sadly misinformed, if not delusional. While chuckling about the parents' estimation of their children's intelligence, I apparently failed to notice my overblown assessment of my own.

What I knew for certain was that there was a significant range of expectations from the parents regarding whether or not to "push" the child during the appointment. At the two extremes of this spectrum were two groups. The first group, which I called the "Get 'er done" group, held the position that completing the appointment at all costs was tantamount. When I had a parent who made that clear to me, it opened the door for me to continue care even in the face of tears and crying by the child. This was never my favorite situation, but for each patient, I knew that I was the dentist and had one vote and the two parents each had one, so that I was outvoted. I will quickly add, though, that this approach never went beyond my own professional ethics. Regardless of how the parents laid out their expectations, if I felt a child simply could not cope with the procedures, I would stop work. If that was unacceptable to the parent, I would invite them to go elsewhere.

The second group at the other extreme end of the spectrum was characterized by their great concern and sensitivity to the child's well-being during the appointment. Their words would more typically fall into the category of "My child is very sensitive and if he says 'peep' I want you to stop treatment immediately." This, too, was helpful going into visits since I knew that calling it a day for a given child would be supported by the parent. The problem with the two groups was that I wasn't skilled enough to delineate between them by the subtleties of their behavior. There were two situations that swayed me into inviting parents into the treatment area during their children's visits. Both occurred when my policy forbade this.

Raquel, my receptionist, came into the treatment area one day and told me that she had received a call about a two-year-old who had bumped a tooth. Any time a child sustained trauma, I would tell the parents to bring the child in for an examination so that I could get a baseline of how the tooth, teeth, or gum tissues were at that moment. In this way I could follow the situation to see if it was improving or getting worse and determine the best plan. Very few minutes later, the child came in. While not unheard of, in 1982 it was a bit unusual for a father to bring a child into the office. I would guess that 95% or more of the children came in with their mother. However, in the case of this little boy, it was his father, who happened to be an Olympia police officer. I'm happy to report that I have had very few occasions to be in the presence of a police officer in full uniform, but this was one of them. He seemed to be a very pleasant man, but I couldn't help noticing that he had a badge, a gun, and a club. When he told me what had happened, I said that we'd take Bradley back, take an x-ray, and let him know. I took the boy from the officer and retreated. My skilled assistant managed the x-ray on this two-year-old, but the result was not happy news. The "bump" turned out to be a significant fracture of the root below the level of bone. That meant that only one procedure could be recommended, that being extraction. I returned to consult with the officer. As always, I tried to imagine what he would say and how he would want me to proceed. I invited him into the consultation room and the visit went like this with each of his comments being both terse and quick:

Officer: So how is Bradley?
Me: He's fine, but his tooth has been injured.
Officer: Yes, I know. Is it bad?
Me: Yes, he fractured the root of his front tooth
Officer: So, what are we going to do about it?

Given his direct responses, I felt I had a sense of which side of the spectrum his expectations would be, but at the same time, his badge seemed shinier at this point, his club seemed longer and fatter and his gun was clearly loaded with bullets. I shifted a bit, nervous to answer the question.

Me: Well, officer, there really is only one option.
Officer: OK, what is it?
Me: Well, uh, we need to extract that tooth

I took a breath to await his response but cast my eyes down toward the floor. He did not answer. When I finally looked up, there were tears coming down his cheeks. I folded my arm over his shoulder and comforted him in spite of my utter surprise at this unexpected reaction. I would have placed lots of money on his saying, "Let's do it." Later I wondered if the tears were for his son or for himself, having to return home to tell his wife that this had occurred to Bradley on his watch. My status as a psychic was in jeopardy.

Zoe, the very bright daughter of Mrs. Cameron, was a new patient and had several cavities that required my attention. Her mother, a soft-spoken woman, explained to me that Zoe was a very, very sensitive child. She continued to recount her own negative dental experiences as a child and made it very clear that if Zoe had any problems at all, she wanted me to stop. A positive experience was the most important thing, according to Mrs. Cameron. I appreciated clarity of this sort, especially when my own confidence in assessing subtle signs had been put in question. The day came for Zoe's appointment, and, as she entered the operatory, the look on her face reminded me of the little red person who sits on your shoulder, telling you to do bad things. I wondered why I couldn't see the pair of red horns sprouting from her head, but I was still ready to make Zoe's appointment a good one. With the placement of the topical anesthetic with the Q-tip, Zoe launched into spluttering and writhing. I didn't get overly concerned, as it was the girl's first visit with us, and everything was new to her. When the injection was attempted, Zoe ramped up her resistance to the point that I was concerned both for her safety as well as for my own, since Mrs. Cameron made her specific goal very clear. I decided using a mild sedative for Zoe would increase the chances of making all of us happier, and I ended the appointment. When I went out to speak with Mrs. Cameron, here is how that conversation went:

Me: Mrs. Cameron, would you please step in?
Mrs. Cameron: Oh, my goodness, Dr. Psaltis, that was so quick.
Me: Well, we didn't complete the filling.
Mrs. Cameron: But how's Zoe doing?
Me: She got a little agitated when we placed the topical anesthetic...
Mrs. Cameron (breaking in): But is she all right?
Me (desperately wishing I could tell her how my staff and I were doing after Zoe's shenanigans, I called up my professional self and responded to the question): She's fine but knowing how much you wanted this to be a

positive experience for her, I decided it was best to stop the appointment and give her a mild sedative so that we can accomplish that positive experience that both you and I want.

At this moment, I felt a surge of pride about being a sensitive male, having listened intently to a mother's explicit instructions and then following through to the tee. Delusions are not common in my life, but what happened next told me once again that my psychic skills were flawed.

Mrs. Cameron (in a crescendo of both volume and exasperation): Do you mean you didn't complete the filling? Do you know that Zoe had to miss class today because you wouldn't see her after school? Do you know that I am missing work to bring her here today? Aren't you the professional here?

Having been a baseball fan all my life, I understood that when we have two strikes against us, the next one will end our turn at bat. Not one to enjoy striking out, I pondered these two nearly consecutive, but polar opposite experiences and decided it was time for a change. I did an about-face from "NEVER" and established parent guidelines so that they could be present during the visit. The only "never" that remained in the policy was never again having to guess at a parent's goal for an appointment. Not only did I solve that problem, but I also discovered that by having the parents witness our care, the degree of gratitude expressed rose enormously. When I had a mother like Mrs. Cameron and the child was beginning to lose control near the end of the appointed time, I could simply look up and ask if she wanted me to continue or reschedule. Even the most adamant proponents of the good experience philosophy would tell me to keep on going. Many would later tell me that they couldn't even brush their own children's teeth and they were flabbergasted that we could place fillings or crowns without difficulty. I would just nod, complete the task and celebrate that I no longer depended on my psychic abilities. Hating to lose my relationship with the silent "p," though, I would recognize that much of my success was doubtless due to my background in psychology.

CHAPTER 4

Must be that midterm

Several factors go into a pediatric dental schedule. The most critical is the age of the patient. Another is the complexity of treatment that is planned. Finally, it is the strength of the dentist, which is just another way of saying, the age of the dentist. I fondly look back on my younger years when I felt able to do anything at any time without difficulty. When I lived on 9.4 acres of land in Olympia, I could literally spend all day Friday, Saturday, and most of Sunday working on the property. I dug postholes by hand, and because of the heavy clay soil that is typical for the coastal areas of Washington State, this was no easy job. I could muscle railroad ties for the fencing, stretch barbed wire, nail it all together, all while still managing to cook my meals and tend to my children. Somewhere in there, I'd take a jog or Nordic Track while watching a recorded television show. On Monday morning, I could hop out of bed, make my beloved cup of coffee, and go back into the office, full of energy. I miss those days. But it wasn't a precipitous drop off into an abyss of weariness. Like much of life, it was a gradual, if not imperceptible change at glacial speed that one can only appreciate after a while when the differences became obvious. When I opened my practice in 1981, I could see patients at any time of the day simply because it was necessary to build the practice. In the earliest days of my career, having eight children on my daily schedule was a delight. It was a reduction from my days in the Navy, but these were paying patients and the thrill of actually receiving compensation based on the work I did was heady and fulfilling.

Different pediatric dentists naturally do things differently. My style of scheduling was rather simple. The day would begin with the youngest patients or the children needing sedation. The third category was those whose treatment plan for the day would be most taxing to both patient and provider, so that we were both maximally rested and ready for the appointment. I always considered this to be so obvious to everyone that the idea of doing anything else never crossed my mind. I also felt that the late afternoon appointments should best be held for my "older" patients, namely those in high school. At this point in their academic careers, they might miss a crucial class, and I was respectful of that. Afternoon appointments were, however, always the most popular since most parents didn't want their children to miss school if possible. That also grew out of the funding of school systems. Districts apparently would be paid according to the number of students in attendance so that policies were set making it more difficult for children to be out of class for reasons other than emergencies. This raised a number of issues for children's dentists. While some general dentists can accommodate the work schedule of adults by appointing them evenings, it is hardly reasonable to consider starting a pediatric dental practice in the afternoon when the majority of the patients to be seen are already tired from their days. A nighttime visit with a three-year-old can only be seen as something between ill-advised and comical.

In spite of all these hurdles, the schedule in my practice typically ran smoothly, with the age of the patients ascending all day long. The very young would be seen in the morning hours, and by the time we had children who were able to write their own names, it was well into that same morning. Afternoon appointments were normally with patients whose ages were in double digits. Families with multiple children also posed a bit of a challenge in that they included children ranging in age from three to fifteen. One family, the Hansons, were the largest in the practice, with ten children. I could hardly imagine dinner time at their table, but that wasn't mine to do. Finding an appropriate time slot for the children was mine to do, however, and we normally compromised by seeing them in smaller groups. I loved that family. The mom was one of the parents I always enjoyed seeing. She brought a smile to my own face whenever her children came in. I would envision scheduling all of her children at one time so that we'd know they had arrived when the Greyhound bus pulled in.

As my practice grew, it eventually reached the point where I would see sixty children per day. Few people outside of my particular specialty can imagine it. Pediatric dentistry is different than general dentistry in that we don't have lengthy appointments for full-mouth reconstruction, for example. Pediatric practices mostly deal with short, simple procedures such as tooth cleaning, fluoride application, and shorter filling visits. A young child's attention span will not always allow an appointment beyond thirty minutes, so at no time was there ever a single lengthy and productive appointment that could make my day. The other factor is that pediatric practices typically have large, dedicated, and talented teams of hygienists and assistants to support the doctors. When I began the practice, the State of Washington was one of the most progressive in terms of training and licensing auxiliaries to do many of the procedures, thus freeing the dentist to both see more children (access to care) and become the primary educa-tor. The definition of "doctor" actually is "teacher." No longer encumbered by all the technical aspects of the direct oral care, I could spend more of my time answering parent questions and sharing the knowledge I had gained through dental school and my years of experience. The women who worked with me were dedicated to their tasks and to the children we saw. I never stopped admiring their caring for the children, even under the worst of circumstances. Perhaps it is that mothering instinct, but even when a child might vomit, it was as if a giant magnet had suddenly been turned on and these women would flock to the scene to clean up the mess, nurture the child, and generally make my life much, much better. I was always grateful.

Because of my team, seeing sixty patients per day was not as challenging as one might think. I became accustomed to the flow and the rhythm and learned to pace myself during the day so that I was ready to provide the same level of focus, care, and professionalism for my final patient of the day as I did for the first. When I was thirty-three years old and seeing eight to ten patients per day, this was very easy. By the time I reached the age of sixty-five and was seeing sixty patients per day, that glacial shift in energy had made itself abundantly clear. It was the pacing that required my attention because rhythm had long since departed my aging body. I relied more heavily on the schedule to treat me as well as I wanted to treat the children. The next layer of scheduling was to have the restorative (filling) visits in the morning when my own focus and strength was highest, and the simpler, checkup appointments in the afternoons. My body told me that an arrangement of this type was best for all. It certainly was for me. Scheduling like this was not often a problem, but occasionally that challenging parent would disrupt my carefully orchestrated day with a request that opposed of my beliefs.

It may seem that parents were often a problem, but that is not really true. The overwhelming majority were cooperative, kind, and often engaging. I enjoyed most of them. Like every category of human being, including dentists, some were problematic for me with their demands or their insistence that they knew more about dentistry than I did. This came from their night-before-the-appointment tutorial from Dr. Google. Misinformation did not begin with the internet, but it got a boost. "Old wives' tales" must have been the earliest manifestation of this. Some people still think the world is flat and that Elvis is still alive. With the acceleration of blogs as a significant source of information, most health-care professionals are now challenged to convince patients that science remains the recommendable source for treatment decisions. However, there is one realm in which the parents had a distinct advantage over me, and it was never clearer to me than when Mrs. Hawkinson came in with Austin.

Austin, himself, was a rather cute and nice child. He was cooperative and generally in good dental health. He was also a typical three-year-old child in terms of his development, his attention span, and his understanding of what we were actually doing. When he presented for his third checkup visit, I found a cavity that required my attention and explained to Mrs. Hawkinson that it would require a morning appointment since that was when we scheduled filling appointments. She said that she very much preferred an afternoon time slot. This led to my scholarly explanation about how younger children typically do far better in the morning when they are well rested so that they can cope with the procedures. Having heard my words Mrs. Hawkinson replied, "Well, Dr. Psaltis, you don't know my son like I do. He usually naps in the morning, and he is an afternoon child. Also, I don't want him to miss school." Who was I to argue? To suggest to a mother that I knew more about a child than she did is clearly not a practice builder. I was curious, though, about one part of her statement. "What school does Austin attend?" I asked. "Pre-school," she stated. In my mind I wondered if the preschool was having a midterm or famous guest speaker that day so that Austin would somehow fall behind or be deprived of something special. Faced with this dilemma I responded with what I knew was my own reality. "Thank you, Mrs. Hawkinson, for that information," I began. "I didn't know that about your boy. However, there is something I feel you need to know about me," I said to her, "I am a morning person."

One of the tightrope acts that I always felt I needed to accomplish was to be both clear and professional. In the world of political correctness, it is not always easy. Parents deserve to seek the care they want for their children. It is their right. However, what they feel is right for their children is not always congruent with my training, philosophy, experience, or knowledge. At no time did I ever want to antagonize or humiliate a parent, but equally important for me was to not accede to wishes that I felt would lead to a poor result. It requires courage to speak one's truth and, as Dr. Thomison, my wonderful mentor from Sacramento, once told me, it is sometimes the best view of a person when he/she is walking out your door for the last time. This is a painful truth. Mrs. Hawkinson scheduled Austin and we completed his care in a routine morning visit. She did not bring him back again. I hope she found a dentist who was an afternoon person for the boy.

CHAPTER 5

Easy to admire, but easy to hate

Four-and-a-half-year-old Randi was referred into our office due to her difficulty cooperating with the family dentist. She presented with a badly infected tooth that would require extraction and a space maintainer so that the permanent tooth would be able to erupt into her mouth five or six years later. Without the space maintainer, the tendency of teeth to drift forward in the mouth would have closed that area. This would block the normal process of the bicuspid making its way into its proper location. Randi displayed little enthusiasm for having me look into her mouth, and I knew this would be a difficult situation. I suggested to her mother that sedation might be necessary. Occasionally in situations of this sort, I was thinking to myself that the sedative might be necessary for me, but of course it was Randi who would be the recipient.

Nitrous oxide, for the many jokes about how dentists use it during lunch hours, is an effective tool to helping children be more comfortable during a dental visit. In my experience, the main benefit of it is that it seems to stretch a child's attention span, so that if a given child could sit still for twenty minutes, I could usually count on thirty minutes of working time with the use of the nitrous oxide. In addition, the patient would have some sensations of floating, dreaming or in some other way not noticing what was happening. I did not use it routinely, but I tended to rely on it for the patients who were having a first time-ever filling appointment. I felt it tipped the situation slightly more in my favor and also gave me cause to suggest something stronger should the nitrous oxide not work well. The only time nitrous oxide was administered to me was at my own dentist's office and I did not like it all. For me it created a sensation of dizziness and loss of control, neither of which I found pleasant. Some of my patients felt the same way and would tell me so. At the end of a nitrous oxide visit, I would ask the child if she/he liked the "magic air," as we called it, and it was far from unanimously praised.

Randi's visit began with the magic air with her father, a firefighter, present. He was very affable and may have been there because fathers were occasionally summoned to attend the visit of a child who was fearful or resistant. It wasn't necessary to be a firefighter. The apparent ingredient was the male chromosome. My experiences of firefighters typically came only when I visited a fire station for some continuing education.

Dentists are required to update their CPR skills each year and normally I would hire someone to come into the practice to provide this training. One year I was away from Olympia on the designated day, so I had to find another way to obtain my certification. I knew that it could be done at the local fire stations, so I called until I found one that was able to schedule me for the class. While it may not be true for every single firefighter, I often notice that they are generally a physically fit group. When I arrived at the fire station, I was offered a tour of the facility and accepted. One of the many impressive features of the station was its gymnasium. It was exactly like the weight room at my local fitness club and was occupied by several grunting and straining firefighters. While I understand why some people would prefer not to be in the dental profession, firefighters and police put themselves in harm's way for a living and must have courage beyond that which I possess. The mere idea of running into a burning building is already enough to rattle me, but to be expected to carry people, pets, or other living things out of that inferno is more than I can imagine. When I picture these people climbing ladders, holding the powerful water hoses, and possibly hefting another living person onto their backs, I can appreciate why they are held in high esteem. It also provides enough insight to understand why they spend a part of their down time in the weight room. As a former cross-country runner, I never used weights as a part of my workout routine, and my body shows that. I had great legs. Arms and chest? Not so much. I do think I'm in good cardiac condition as my heart rate and blood pressure are both excellent, but these are not visual aspects that may draw the admiration of others. In short, when I see men who have a physique that is so much more muscular and attractive than mine, I tend to get a jealous. As a matter of fact, I may even find myself quietly hating them because they have proven that it is possible to look like that. Lifting a mouth mirror all day would hardly count as curling reps. It is no wonder that I have never in my life seen a "dentist calendar." It is unlikely that the popularity of a calendar of dentists with their shirts off just wouldn't attract investors. We'll leave those calendars to the firefighters and to them I can only say, "congratulations."

MJ holding Randi after the injection (Father in hat)

With some verbal encouragement to breathe the magic air, Randi started sniffing it and began to calm down a bit. The topical anesthetic went onto her cheek area in her mouth, and all was fine up to this point. The injection was what turned things back toward the negative. I pride myself on giving excellent, pain-free injections, but I am never the recipient of my own work. Success is only measured by the patient's response, and, in Randi's case, it was the opposite of what I had wanted. She was very clear about her dislike of it and MJ, my assistant, was quick to get Randi into her lap and soothe the girl's misery. Tears flowed. Screams filled the room. Dad was there for the entire thing. I recalled that this is a man who could have picked me up and carried me out of the room because of his weight training at the fire station.

I was unhappy knowing that the girl felt pain during the injection. I was also a bit nervous about Randi's father. He certainly seemed like a very kind man, but knowing how I, myself, am prepared to go to war with anybody who hurts my own children, I could only smile and weakly tell him, "We'll wait to make sure she is very numb before we begin." I was already partially numb.

With MJ's brilliant work, Randi did calm down and I managed to get the anesthetic in the right spot. Few people (other than dentists) realize or even want to think about the fact that all injections are essentially done blind. Landmarks exist for the start of the needle penetration, but once the tip has disappeared, it cannot be watched up to the final place where the nerve ending is hiding. With years of experience, professionals become very adept at this, but the variation in the shapes of mouths and bodies makes it all but impossible to place the anesthetic correctly each and every time. Still another advantage of working with children is the fact that the target area is smaller than in adults, so the likelihood of our efforts being successful is greater. In Randi's case, she amply demonstrated the effectiveness by tapping on her lower lip, trying to bite it, and expressing that amazement that comes with the odd feeling of numbness. We were ready to go to work.

Extractions of primary teeth are not always simple. The public, which has only experienced a baby tooth either falling out or being removed by a child or parent, is often not even aware of the fact that they have roots. The natural process of baby tooth loss is that specialized cells in the body called *cementoclasts* have the unique job of literally eating away the layers of root structure on primary teeth. In this way, when a permanent successor tooth is ready to emerge into the child's mouth, there is no longer anything holding its predecessor in place. Cementoclasts are like Pac-man, gnawing away these roots. This explains why the teeth become loose and, when sitting in the palm of somebody's hand, have no roots on it. The roots did exist earlier and if an extraction of a primary molar is required, the roots can be quite fragile, curved or in some other way shaped so that their removal is never a routine procedure. I always told the children that they would feel *squeezing* but shouldn't feel any *pain*. This, I would demonstrate by squeezing on one of their fingers and asking if they could feel the squeezing. They would always say "yes." I would then ask them if they could feel any pain and they would typically say "no." "That is how it will feel when I wiggle your tooth," I would say as I finished the preparation for the extraction.

Several specific steps are necessary for the extraction of any tooth, but with primary teeth, I always felt it was important to go very slowly, carefully, and not exert too much pressure at any given moment. I never wanted to hear a snap that would indicate that a root had broken under the pressure of my forceps. With nervous children like Randi, all those same elements went into the procedure for the well-being of the child. It was clear to me that the girl was entirely numb as I began to manipulate the abscessed tooth back and forth several times to loosen it so that I could easily lift it out of the socket. Ironically for extractions, there is often far more *pushing* involved than *pulling*. Still, the common phrase of "pulling teeth" remains a part of most people's vocabulary, including the phrase well known for measuring the extreme difficulty of anything being "as hard as pulling a tooth." Actually, I push until I can lift.

Randi did just fine as my constant monologue was much like a baseball play-by-play, which was my dream job. Maybe that's why I always enjoyed giving the patients my own version of what was happening. It was my way of wishing I were calling a baseball game. There is a moment when it's clear that the tooth can be lifted out because of the degree of looseness that I created. When it departed Randi's mouth, I used one of my favorite tricks. With the tooth now safely wrapped in a gauze pad in my assistant's hand, I would ask the child, "Are you ready for me to take the tooth out now?" They would say that they were ready and at that moment I would tell them that it was already out. Eyes bugged, brow knitted, Randi just stared at me with that "Are you kidding me?" look on her face. I delighted in this little game, particularly for the benefit of the parent sitting next to the child. They, too, expressed their surprise at the ease of the procedure. If I may, I must add here that it isn't magic. It's experience and knowledge, but no matter what it was, the result was invariably marvelous.

Randi at the end of her visit

One of the differences between mothers and fathers is the degree to which most men openly express feelings. It is typically far less than women. I don't go to work to be showered with accolades all day long, so it never bothered me if neither parent said much after a child's appointment. When a man let his emotions out, it was notable, as with the police officer previously described. So it was with Randi's dad. As I have explained, he was a very kind man, but frankly intimidating with his physique. At the end of Randi's visit, as she smiled lopsidedly due to the numb lower lip, her father looked at her, then looked at me. He then looked at her again and looked at me. I wasn't sure what to expect, but at last his pondering of whether or not to become emotional brought him to the pregnant moment. He looked at Randi one final time and looked back at me. I knew something was up and I was both curious and slightly concerned about what might happen next. As it turned out, there was no need to worry. He took a step toward me and allowed himself to pour his feelings out to me by extending his hand and quietly saying, "Thanks, man." I had an emotional moment of my own in witnessing this touching moment of male emotion. If my house ever catches on fire, I hope he will be the one who carries me out. I'll look at my house, look at him, look at my house, look at him and finally extend my hand and scream, "YOU SAVED MY LIFE, MAN!!"

CHAPTER 6

We're not going to talk about that today

My role as a child's dentist was to advise parents about what I felt was the best care possible, and then it was up to the parents to decide if they would pursue that or not. I was fortunate to practice prior to the internet boom and also at a time when both science and the opinion of a health care professional were respected. On one hand, it may seem as though that would be the ideal era to practice dentistry since there was less disagreement, less frustration, and a greater ease in saying exactly what needed to be done. On the other hand, it placed a greater burden of responsibility on me to be up to date with my knowledge, take the many gray-area factors into consideration, and make a responsible and correct recommendation to the parent for a child. During my career, most parents would accept my treatment plans and suggestions and, as far as I could tell, the children typically benefitted from my knowledge.

There were often small areas of disagreement, such as with fluoride. Since the health benefits of fluoride had been scientifically established, I was always amazed at the degree of resistance some people had toward it. When I first moved to Olympia to become the second children's dentist in the area, the local dental society saw an opportunity for the "new guy in town" to be the face of its campaign to get the city of Olympia fluoridated.

Still naïve and fresh from the Navy, where very little controversy existed since officers made all the calls, I felt this opportunity would give me good exposure to the community. I could just imagine the kudos I would receive for my work to bring a greater level of health to the children of my new town. Little did I know at that time what came with the assignment.

I spent time with the chairman of the Department of Pediatric Dentistry at the University of Washington in Seattle to gather facts that simply couldn't fail to sway the opinion of everyone. On the night that the city council met to have an open forum regarding the proposal to fluoridate the city, I was slightly nervous, but mostly eager to share my expansive knowledge on the topic. The format of the evening was that each person who wanted to speak had to sign in on a sheet of paper and indicate whether they were in favor or opposed to the action. My first sniff of the problem was staring at the rapidly growing list of names on the "opposed" side of the sheet. Still confident that I could hold sway, I took my seat. Each person would have only two minutes to speak, and the sides would alternate—those for, and those against. I was not the first person to speak on the "in favor" side, but some of the information being shared was in my warehouse of data. I had no fear. I was packed with facts. When my turn finally came, I gave my best two-minute spiel about the incidence of decay in the children of Washington State, the effectiveness of fluoride in the water, and the low cost of such a valuable public health measure. Satisfied, I took my seat again and, for the next hour or so, listened with shock and amazement at the arguments leveled by the foes. They included:

- Why should we water our flowers with fluoride?

- If fluoride is so good for you, why don't you eat a pound of it?

- I don't want any chemicals in my water

- If children would just brush their teeth, there would be no decay

- My tax dollars should go to something more important

- Fluoride is a poison, and I don't want to be poisoned

- People go insane if they have too much of the stuff

All of this debate was before the internet was enabling people to gather any information they wanted as long as it agreed with their own point of view. There may be no "drug" (actually, it's an element) that has been more thoroughly studied than fluoride. The first community to be fluoridated was Grand Rapids, Michigan, and the only large-scale result of the implementation was a marked decrease in tooth decay. There was no insanity, flowers flourished, and it seemed that nobody died from it. Missing from the body of knowledge of those opposed was the fact that their public water supply already had chemicals in it, namely chlorine. It is of the same group of elements (known as halogens) as fluorine. Also lacking was the understanding that most table salt contains iodine, still another of the halide group, and, when, taken in microscopic amounts, prevents goiter. To understand these connections, it is not always easy if one fails to understand science, a problem with which we are still dealing.

In fairness, I will quickly add that I know other professionals (including dentists) who are very much opposed to fluoride and many other materials used in dentistry. Some have confronted me in the middle of one of my lectures, and others have sent me masses of material which, in their opinion, shows the faults of fluoride. At some point in my maturation process, I realized that I am not the font of all knowledge. I am also not arrogant enough to believe that I am always right, and that others are always wrong. I had a relationship with a person like that for years and became exhausted by the arguments, so I ultimately modified my dental beliefs to allow room for other opinions even if I didn't agree. However, I do not allow others to dictate to me what I must do, particularly if it opposes my own ethics and knowledge.

Back to the fluoride campaign. To my surprise, the campaign failed. The vote was very close, but it went down by something like 50.8% to 49.2%. That was a surprise, but nothing like the shock I received when I began opening threatening letters at my office. The letters were unsigned, but they made it clear that "if I continued to push for the poison in the Olympia water system, I had better watch out." As the father of a newborn daughter, this particularly upset me, as it was my first taste of what it must be like to be a public figure. Once the vote was in and the referendum failed, the letters stopped coming, but I can only imagine how it might be in today's world, in which the internet makes contacting others so simple.

Fortunately, I never encountered anything quite as dramatic in my practice, but I did have some parents who were opposed to some of my policies or the treatment recommendations I made. None of them sent me nasty letters, but a few of them left the practice. Initially I found this very distressing. It was hard to not take it personally, but with time I recognized that parents are also doing the best they can for their children, so certain decisions must ultimately be left up to them. When I became a parent, I appreciated more deeply how parents are protective of their children. As long as their requests (or demands) didn't cross any lines in my judgment, I could remain flexible.

Mrs. Whatcom was one of my most challenging parents in this regard. Her daughter, Isabella, was a delightful, engaging girl who started in my practice at about the age of seven years. As with all my patients, I saw her every six months for a checkup visit and to monitor her dental and facial growth and development. I did not treat Isabella or Mrs. Whatcom differently than any other patient/parent dyad, but I encountered more resistance from the mother about my treatment recommendations. She balked at sealants for her daughter's permanent molars, maintaining that Isabella had excellent home care and didn't need any "protection" from decay. She opted out of a fluoride prescription for the same reason. These were classic examples of a parent disagreeing in a fashion that didn't force me to defile my own standards. I presented the plans in the most informative and understandable way I could, and the parent said no. There was no harm done in these instances since it was not an active avoidance of something crucial. That was one of my benchmarks—are the parents refusing care that is likely to create a problem in the future? If that were the case, I would simply ask them to leave the practice since I felt my knowledge and recommendations didn't match their own. Under those circumstances, it was my opinion that they would be happier in a practice that was more in sync with themselves.

When Isabella turned fifteen, I recommended a panoramic x-ray that would give me the opportunity to evaluate her developing third molars, more commonly called the "wisdom teeth." In her case, I could clearly see that they were growing horizontally in the bone so that there was literally no chance they would erupt into the girl's mouth properly. The best plan was to have them removed before the roots became too long, which would complicate the procedure in the future. At the end of Isabella's visit, I took a copy of the x-ray, along with a referral slip to an oral surgeon, and asked Mrs. Whatcom to come in for the consultation. Having had experience with her, I began with all the good news—her daughter had no cavities and no obvious orthodontic needs. To this, the mother smiled, and I suspected she was thinking that my report proved her to be correct about Isabella not needing fluoride or sealants. When I then began discussing her wisdom teeth, Mrs. Whatcom stopped me at the moment I said the words "wisdom teeth" and told me that nothing needed to be done about them. She and her husband both still had their wisdom teeth and never needed to have them removed. She was very clear in telling me that we weren't going to talk about that today.

Six months later Isabella was back and once again at the end of her appointment, I called Mrs. Whatcom in for consultation. The report was the same as before, no cavities and no need for braces and oh, by the way, did you happen to think any more about those wisdom teeth? This was nothing more than fulfilling my responsibility to my patient by discussing all aspects of her oral health. Now slightly piqued, the woman glared at me and again said to me, "We're not going to talk about that today." I got the message and remembered my own realization that my job is to inform. Parents' job is to decide. The vote for extraction of the wisdom teeth was one to one, but I was fairly certain that Mr. Whatcom might not want to get into it with her. Besides, it was most often true that the mothers were the decision makers for the children's needs. I was still convinced that the teeth would create havoc for the girl, but I had performed my duty to inform her mother of Isabella's situation.

We're not going to talk about that today

A year had passed since the x-ray and six months since the last encounter, but now I knew that based on my experience, the roots of those teeth had lengthened and with each passing day, week and month, the difficulty of removing those impacted teeth would increase. The person who would suffer would be Isabella. I decided I'd try a different tactic this time. It wasn't that I wanted to be sneaky, but rather that I wanted to be an advocate for the child and make it as clear as possible that this was a problem that required attention, either now or later, and the latter would be far worse for Isabella. I called Mrs. Whatcom in for still another consultation and began as I always did. This time, my presentation was different, though. I said to her, "Isabella has no cavities, her teeth look nice and straight and we are NOT going to talk about her wisdom teeth today." She looked at me with a slightly puzzled look on her face and asked me if it was important to discuss them. "In my opinion it is," I replied, "but I know you were very clear with me that you didn't want to talk about it." "But should we?" she asked. "That is entirely up to you, Mrs. Whatcom," I told her. After a pause, she said that she wanted to understand what was going on in her daughter's mouth. I brought out the one-year-old x-ray and showed her how the teeth were growing horizontally in the bone and had no chance at all to upright themselves and grow into Isabella's mouth. She again told me that both she and husband never had their wisdom teeth removed and that she just couldn't understand what she was looking at. I did my best to explain variations in tooth size and jawbone size and that in Isabella's case, there would be no room for the teeth even if they came in straight. I could nearly hear the wheels turning in Mrs. Whatcom's head, but I finally heard the words I had hoped to hear a year earlier. "OK, give me a referral slip, and we'll check with the oral surgeon," she said.

Six months later at her checkup visit I asked Isabella if she'd gotten her wisdom teeth out. She told me yes, they had been removed, and the oral surgeon told her mother that it was a good thing they were taken out because they would have been a serious problem if the extractions had been delayed. When I called Mrs. Whatcom in for her semi-annual consultation, I told her that Isabella had no cavities, would not need orthodontics, and I ended my report. What I knew in my heart was that if I had broached the topic of the wisdom teeth, Mrs. Whatcom most likely would have said to me, "We're not going to talk about that today." Luckily for Isabella, she didn't need to say it.

CHAPTER 7

Extended family—Part II

Olympia is neither a big city nor a small town. It is somewhere in between, and that fact alone is a reason I like it here. There's much to do within a short distance—ski in the Cascades, go clamming on the Pacific beaches, and hike in Mount Rainier National Park just to name a few. In my case, I can also kayak from my back yard. Our home sits on the shores of one of the Puget Sound inlets so a one-minute walk from our house to the water makes it easy to be paddle on saltwater with seals, starfish, herons, and other wonderful wildlife around me. Olympia's historic downtown has morphed into an interesting place to meander, and the Farmers Market is the second biggest in the entire state, trailing only the famed Pike Place Market in Seattle. The state capitol grounds provide an air of importance while the Tugboat Festival on Budd Bay on the edge of downtown reminds us of the laid-back atmosphere that also prevails.

All of that is enough to make life in Olympia enjoyable, but the fact that the population is just enough for sufficient anonymity, yet small enough for familiarity, feels almost perfect. I wonder at how it is possible to attend a play in town and not recognize a single person in the audience, and yet have other moments when I feel that I know everybody. Having cared for thousands of children is a source for many of my adult connections in town and, occasionally, out of town.

The focus in my practice was always on the patients, but some of the parents who brought them became still another extended family for me. It was not only from patients that I received hugs. In fact, the great majority of the hugs came from grateful mothers. Some were with tearful eyes after a successful dental visit when worries had dominated the moms' pre-appointment thoughts, only to be replaced by emotional responses of relief and gratitude. Others came from some of the engaging mothers that came in and, over time, became like friends. Although I sometimes wondered if any of them felt it was inappropriate to give me a hug, women are not typically questioned for delivering a spontaneous hug. More important, the hug, itself, lent even more credence to my belief that I had a family within the practice. I do not, for example, walk up to people on the sidewalk and give them hugs. Personally, I like hugs. It is a way to express a sentiment. With texting, emailing, Snapchat and other digital communications, face-to-face conversations have become rarer pleasures for all of us. In the same way, during the COVID pandemic, any form of touching other than with elbows was taboo. Masks reduced our ability to share facial expressions. For me, I treasure the times when parents shared a hug with me.

Hugs aren't the only way I measure that sense of extended family, though. When I needed an MRI for a shoulder problem, I sat in the curtained alcove with the embarrassing tie-in-the-back drape covering me. A friendly medical tech pulled the curtain back, looked at me and exclaimed, "Dr. Psaltis!" This occurred during the pandemic and her face was covered so that I had minimal visual clues, but it took only a moment for Cheryl Ann to happily announce, "You were my children's dentist." This is always a welcome phrase as long as it is not being snarled. "I brought my children in to your office for many years," she continued, "and one of them was an unhappy-faced patient that you got through his visits."

Not every parent was quite as familiar with me. Mothers and fathers are quite different that way. Each Monday morning a group of retired men gather over a long cup of coffee to talk, laugh, share, and generally do what guys do. I was invited to join the group by a friend, Rolf, who saw my wife and me walking down a local road. He stopped and we chatted, and he suggested I might enjoy joining his "coffee group." He told me the time and place where the men met, and I decided I'd go. I had spent thirty-six years in private practice, and during that time had a total of one male employee. He lasted about two weeks before taking another job. The majority of my patients were accompanied by their mothers. There were exceptions, but if I were to put a number on it, I'd say 90% or more of the children were brought by their moms. In short, I was hungry for some male companionship. Having spent years meeting new people in my practice, I was a bit surprised that I felt nervous about encountering an unknown group of people. Rolf was not there, so it was up to me to grab a chair, sit down and dig right in. I introduced myself and explained how Rolf had told me about the group. I quickly felt at ease. The men next to me engaged me in conversation, thus breaking the ice. As introductions around the table were made, one of the men said, "My name is Andy McMurtry." I am blessed with a good memory. I always tell people that it is not because I do exercises to enhance or expand it. I was simply born with it. I got my brown eyes and the bald head gene from my mom, and I was also blessed with a good memory. Lucky me. "McMurtry?" I asked. "Do you happen to know a Jonah McMurtry?" I posed. Andy looked at me, smiled and replied, "Yes, he's my son. How do you know him?" When I explained that I had been Jonah's dentist, Andy said something to the effect of "Oh, so YOU are the guy I'd write checks to." A father's perspective versus Cheryl Ann's again demonstrated one of the differences between moms and dads, but also provided a way to connect instantaneously with Andy.

Occasionally there were times I would be walking in town, perhaps at the Tugboat Festival, Farmers Market, at a local grocery store or just down a sidewalk and a couple would be approaching me. My memory would kick in and I would recognize the face of the woman as a mother in my practice so that I broke out in a smile to confirm that I knew who she was. This was often generic. In spite of my fortunate memory, I didn't always recall every person's name as I did for Andy's son. The women often returned the smile and offered a "hi" to me as they passed. I only wished I could do a U-turn and listen to the conversation that followed, as the husband may have wondered just who that man was that just exchanged pleasantries with his wife.

My wife and I began vacationing in Cabo San Lucas in 1993. Our son was four months old at the time, and we reveled in the fact that he flipped over from his stomach to his back for the first time at the Sol Mar Hotel. It was a marker event. We ultimately made it our annual vacation spot each February so that we could bask in the sunshine and warmth while taking a break from the Pacific Northwest grayness of winter.

As we returned from an evening's meal one night, I felt a hand slap against my shoulder unexpectedly, and, when I turned to see who had tapped me, I recognized the man as the father of a patient. As was often the case with many parents, I didn't know *his* name, but l instantly recalled his son's, so that I could blurt out, "So how is Zane?" I felt this established that I knew with whom I was speaking, even though I had no clue about his name. This was similar to my situation with Andy in the coffee group, and I was pleased that I could pull it off. In this case, though, John, as I ultimately discovered, engaged me as if he'd known me for years. I was surprised that he was aware of who I was. As it turned out, his wife had pointed me out to him. John was there with four other golfers and asked if I'd like to join them. I had often thought of playing a round of golf in Cabo, given the gorgeous courses there, but I wasn't enough of a golfer to pursue it on my own. As it turned out, the golf day was barely short of a disaster. I quickly learned that the other men, unlike me, were serious golfers. John made it easier on me by saying that he was a "hacker" and we both agreed to end our game at the 13th hole. We were tired of walking through the desert looking for our misplayed shots.

Because I was in practice in Olympia for more than thirty years, I'm not sure why it surprised me that some of the "referrals" were not really referrals at all. They were repeat patients, not per se, but rather the children of previous patients. When new patients were the children of former patients, it was special to me. It was initially a novelty until finally I saw enough of them that I dubbed them, "grandpatients." While gratifying, it was not without some challenges. On several occasions, I would finish my examination of new patient and tell her, "Maddie, you have no sugar bugs today, and I am proud of you for holding your head so still for me." Once the appointment was clearly at an end, the father would pipe up and say, "Maddie, Dr.

Psaltis was my dentist when I was your age." Even though I felt obligated to recall the parent as a former child in my practice, the problem was that I would look up at the father and see a man with a full beard. This was far from his appearance when he was a patient. I would desperately search my memory bank for any clue about who this person was. Unless he had stuck his tongue out at me, or given me tie as a good-bye gift, it was difficult to recall a name from the thousands of patients I had seen. Still, the message I took home was one of gratitude. They sometimes commented, "I want my child to have the same experiences I had as a child in your practice."

Dr. Psaltis was my dentist when I was your age

Whether at a medical facility, at a coffee house, during a stroll through town, on a golf course, or in my own dental building, the sense of family reminded me that the parents, much like their children, had created an extended family for me. With the newest additions, my dental family had expanded to another generation.

CHAPTER 8

Letters from parents

One of the things I miss in our now-digitally dominated world is a written letter. I recall how I would open my tiny mailbox at Stanford University and eagerly pull out those envelopes that contained someone's personal handwriting, as well as their thoughts, feelings, and questions. My dad was my most faithful correspondent, as his weekly ritual included sitting down each Sunday night and writing me a letter long hand. I would write back to him in the same format. Long distance calls cost too much then, and, since we were 840 miles apart, a quick drop-in was not an option. My father never owned a typewriter and died prior to the computer age, so pen and paper made up his media. I loved those letters even if they goaded me into working harder for good grades. It was a connection that included physical objects that each of us touched. These days I don't write letters anymore. I text, I email, and I Snapchat. Only very rarely do I put a pen to paper, usually for a thank you card, still another relic from the past. There is something about the literal contact of a letter that cannot be replaced by a digital version.

It was not common to receive letters from parents in my practice, but they occasionally showed up. Sometimes they were less-than-desired. Once, an angry father wrote to me about a fee that had been charged for care of his daughter. He explained that he felt he had not been informed about the treatment rendered. He insisted that the co-pay be reversed since he had not consented to the treatment or the fee. I appreciated his concerns and his willingness to write to me. In other cases, people would simply leave the practice and we would never know why, although I suspect it was mostly due to fees. In the case of this father, I wrote back to him thanking him for his letter and the fact that it seemed to tell me that the practice needed to communicate more effectively with the parents about treatment. All of that was true. It was also true that his wife had signed the consent form which included the planned care and the fees involved. My words were not belligerent, but they were clear. I included the signed consent form but told him that I would make sure to reverse the charges to which he objected. About a week later I received a second letter from him saying that he was impressed by my response and that he, upon checking with his wife, discovered that everything I had written was correct. She had, in fact, signed the consent, and he was unaware of that. He concluded his letter by insisting that he remit the co-payment. It was not my goal, but it was the result. I do wonder if I had phoned him and presented the information verbally if he could have taken in the facts. In the letter, he had a tangible piece of information that he could digest at his own pace, and the result was that he came to a better understanding of the situation. I was prepared to write off the fee in the fashion of the Nordstrom philosophy of "the customer is always right," but by responding compassionately, yet clearly, it led to the unexpected result because, I believe, it was a letter.

Another letter that arrived early in my career came from a mother of three girls. She lived in a community that was about a half hour away from Olympia, and the children were not referred into my practice by a dentist. I eventually found out that a friend of hers, who also had children in my practice, had recommended the practice to the woman.

```
Gregory L. Psaltis D.D.S.
222 Lilly Road N.E.
Olympia, WA 98506


July 29, 1988


Dear Dr. Psaltis & Staff;

        About 2 months ago I brough my daughter Michelle in for her
first check-up.  I was referred to your office by
                    The visit was explained to me on the phone and I
was asked to pay ½ up front until the insurance claim was processed.
I received information in the mail and confirmation of my appoint-
ment.  I must admit that I was nervous as my girls are not too well
with doctors and are shy with men.

        I tried to prepare Michelle the morning of the visit and I
grew more nervous by the minute.  I imagined the nurses asking me
to come and get her because she was crying and wouldn't let anyone
near her.  Much to my surprise the visit went the exact opposite.
The lady that took her back was very pleasant and I didn't hear
any crying.  Her picture showed a little concern but nothing like
what I imagined.  Dr Psaltis then spent some time with me explaining
the visit and problems that may arise with her teeth in the future.
I left the office feeling very well taken care of and Michelle with
a new bottle for her doll.  She bragged about her visit to her
sister and all her friends at the day care.  I then made an appt.
for my other daughter Jennifer and it also went very well.

        I would like to compliment all of you for the professional
manner in which we were treated.  When the claim was processed and
you received your check, I was issued a refund promptly.  The
entire staff was very friendly and helpful.  You turned what
could have been a disaster into a pleasant event.  I am looking
forward to our 6 month check up in December, and when our baby is
old enough you can be sure she will be in too.

        I do wish you also took adults for the chicken adults like
me.  My imagination probably started from the experiences I have
had with dentists.


Sincerely,
```

This letter provides credence to my observation about adults and dentistry. In particular, I like the sentence "I tried to prepare Michelle the morning of the visit and I grew more nervous by the minute." Equally compelling was her final paragraph, which states, "I do wish you also took adults for the chicken adults like me. My imagination probably started from the experiences I have had with dentists." One might assume that this woman was the anomaly, but, in fact, I heard variations on that theme numerous times from parents sitting in my practice and speaking directly to me. It always reminded me to do all I could to facilitate children's entry into the world of dentistry in the kindest way possible.

Still another letter that touched me came from the mother of Elisha (Elly), described earlier. As I have pointed out, she was a special patient and one whose name I always looked forward to seeing on my daily schedule. Her mother was no less wonderful, and we often chatted during Elly's visits when the girl was still young. As was often the case, Mrs. Fontaine opted out of coming into the office with her daughter once Elly was able to drive and sign her own consent forms. I missed her. I can still recall some of the conversations we had about life, health, and other very human things. Just as her daughter was among my favorite patients, Mrs. Fontaine was among my favorite parents. While I had many I fully enjoyed, some simply stood out.

Dear Dr. Psaltis —
What memories we've shared over the years!!! That little blind girl that was so apprehensive about going to the dentist has grown up to be confident + self-assured — with a beautiful smile! Thank you for your gentle spirit that led her to feel safe going to the dentist. Thank you for your kindness + caring + for the great dental care you have given Elly all these years. She has been lucky to be part of your "Dental Family" for her growing up years.
Blessings + much happiness to you + your family, always + forever — ♡ Lynette (+ Elly) ♡

June 16, 2009

When Elly graduated from high school and sent me her senior picture, Mrs. Fontaine sent me this note expressing her gratitude. Unlike the two letters described above, this one was quite specific about emotions and the results of having had her daughter in my practice for so many years. The phrases that struck me in this note were, "Thank you for your gentle spirit that led her to feel safe going to the dentist" and "She has been lucky to be a part of your 'Dental Family' for her growing up years."

I have a file of letters and notes like the ones described here, but these three most accurately represent the many I received. These letters and notes have shown me that there are many ways to provide health care. It is unfortunate that "the times" have apparently dictated efficiency above all else, because, when "time is money," very little of it is spent on developing these heart-warming relationships. Even the letter from the angry father ultimately proved to be a positive connection with a parent.

It is only in my "senior years" that I more fully appreciate my own father's letters. I sometimes regret not spending more time writing back to him, but I do my best to recognize that my own focus during my Stanford years was gaining an education and moving on toward the next phase of my life. Having had three children away at college, I also realize that I may not have been quite so rigorous in my letter-writing or emailing. While regrets may surface, my musings also bring me to greater understandings. Now I can sit back and genuinely appreciate the letters I received from parents, including my own.

CHAPTER 9

Rules are meant to be broken

Tanya was an eleven-year-old girl when she was referred into my office. She was about to undergo orthodontic treatment but had over-retained primary molars. That means that the previously described *cementoclasts* were not doing their job. Usually, these clever little cells would feast on the roots of primary teeth until the roots were fully resorbed or gone. At that point in time, the teeth would no longer remain in the child's mouth and would also no longer be in the way of the permanent teeth that would succeed them. At times, this just didn't work that way. So it was for Tanya. She still possessed all eight of her primary molars which, by this time in her life, should have been claimed by the tooth fairy. Like many children, Tanya was fearful of the prospect of having her teeth extracted. Perhaps it was the horror stories that float through the ether, or maybe a misplaced word or two from a parent. Whatever the reason, Tanya expressed no enthusiasm for having the procedure completed. In the world of general dentistry, this is called a referral. Often sympathetic to those pediatric dentists who would inherit these children, some of my referring dentists have approached me and literally apologized for sending Donnie or Nicole into my office. I'm sure they possessed the same level of fear of treating these children as the children did of being treated.

I had read the referral slip and studied the x-rays before entering the new patient room to evaluate the situation. These would be very simple extractions since the roots had, to a large degree, been lunch for the *cementoclasts*. Sadly, the meal had not been finished. There were still spicules of root that tenaciously hung on, primarily to the gingival tissues (gums). I expected the teeth to be mobile since those spicules were not anchored in the bone. Even before I had the opportunity to meet the girl, I knew what the problem must be. No dentist would quake at the prospect of removing teeth like these. It had to be the child's fear factor that had triggered the referral. Little did I know how correct my assessment was.

Tanya came in with her father, a burly man with a friendly demeanor. He greeted me as I stepped into the new patient room. Tanya, on the other hand, huddled in the corner, literally pressed against the walls at their juncture. She had her hands over her face. After the introductions and niceties were completed, I began my one-way conversation with Tanya.

Me: "Good morning, Tanya."
Tanya: No response, either verbal or physical
Me: "It looks like you are worried about being here today. Is that true?"
Tanya: Again, no response
Me: "I'm guessing you know why you are here and what needs to be done, right?"
Tanya: The same non-response
Me: "I've looked at the pictures of your teeth and I bet they're loose. Are they?"
Tanya: The pattern was set-- no movement and no words spoken

Now more clearly aware of the degree of fear or worry that the girl possessed, I knew I had to shift gears into a different mode.

Me: "Tanya, did you know that in this office we only treat children?"
Tanya: The same
Me: "Do you know why that is?"
Tanya: No reply
Me: "We only treat children because they are better patients than adults."
Tanya: No reaction

Me: "That's why we won't treat your father. He probably isn't as good a patient as you are."
Tanya: A small, but audible giggle
Me: "Isn't that right, Dad?"

The father, understanding my strategy, gamely said, "Yeah, probably true." With that, Tanya turned to look at him, and laughed out loud.

Me: "So, Tanya, I have seen your teeth in the pictures (x-rays), but I'd like to look at them in your mouth."
Tanya: "Do I need to sit in the chair?"
Me: "No, you can just walk up, and I'll look into your mouth while you stand in front of me."
Tanya: "So I don't have to sit in the chair?"
Me: "No, you do not."

The girl, now at least communicating with me, walked toward me warily. Her body language oozed worry and fear. She finally reached the point directly in front of me and opened her mouth so that I could look into it. In fact, it was very difficult to look into the mouth of a child standing in front of me, but I went through the motions of "um-ing and aha-ing" as I looked up and down into her mouth. It actually made no difference to me since I had seen the x-rays and knew exactly what an oral exam would show.

Me: "Tanya, thanks for opening for me. That was very brave. I have some good news for you and a surprise."
Tanya: "What's the surprise?"
Me: "Well, Tanya, first the good news. I know you are worried about me wiggling your teeth, but by seeing them in your mouth and in the pictures, I'm very confident that this will be much easier than you are thinking. The surprise is that you were so brave to let me look into your mouth, I am going to break one of the office rules for you."
Tanya: "What do you mean, break an office rule?"
Me: "Do you see the pictures of me and the other two doctors on the wall?"
Tanya: "Yes."
Me: "The office rule is that when a patient needs an appointment,

whoever of the three of us has the first appointment available will see that patient. Because you let me look into your mouth, I am going to break the rule and make sure that you get an appointment with me so that I can make sure your appointment is easy."

Tanya: "You would do that for me?"

Me: "Absolutely. Dad, is it all right if I take Tanya to the front desk to arrange that?"

The father, who was now mildly amused but equally grateful, nodded his head yes. I took Tanya to the front desk and introduced her to Raquel.

"Raquel, this is Tanya. Do you know what she did today?" I asked her. Knowing how the office functioned, Raquel was ready to go along and asked me what the girl had done. I told her, "Tanya didn't want me to look in her mouth, but she changed her mind and opened anyway. As a result, I could examine the loose teeth that I need to wiggle at her next visit." Raquel chimed in, "Congratulations, Tanya, you must be a brave girl." The child was now beaming. Me: "Because she IS a brave girl, I want to break an office rule, Raquel. I want you to schedule her with me, even if I am not the person with the next available appointment." Raquel: "I'd be happy to do that. Let's look for a time."

Within moments, a possible appointment time was found, and Tanya and I returned to the new patient room. I advised her father of the date and time and that I would be in the office to care for his daughter. I also recommended use of nitrous oxide to allay some of Tanya's worries. I added that I didn't expect her to be overly concerned now, and that I genuinely felt that the procedure would be far easier than she expected. I'm normally cautious about making guarantees, but given the girl's receptiveness, I had confidence that she would do fine. It is also a strategy of mine to foreshadow the next appointment with a positive outlook for both the child and for me.

When Tanya came in for the first round of extractions, which would be the four lower baby molars, she still was still a bit tentative. The nitrous oxide had its expected effect of calming her, and I approached the girl with my usual soft, reassuring and encouraging manner. The appointment was a breeze. The child was thrilled, her dad was equally happy, and I asked

Tanya if she felt she would be all right seeing one of the other doctors since my next appointment was quite a long time away. She said she would.

Purely by coincidence, I happened to stop by the office the day of Tanya's appointment to get the four upper primary molars removed. I stepped into the room and received an enormous smile, plus a dose of positive energy from the girl. Her father, who accompanied her to each visit, then made a statement to me about how it felt to have his daughter treated in such a way. I listened intently, and then asked him if he would be willing to let me record his words. He asked why I wanted that. I told him that I discuss gratitude in my lectures and his comments fit right in. When he told me it would be fine, I asked him to do his best to say exactly the same thing without any embellishments. He said he'd do his best and, in fact, it was nearly verbatim. This is what he said:

"Previously, my daughter, she had pretty high anxiety when dealing with any dental work or anything like that. Our previous dentist didn't do any kind of nitrous work. We were referred to Small to Tall because they specialize in the pediatric side of dentistry. From the minute we walked in here, the experience has been nothing but pleasant. They worked with my daughter to ease her fears. She's gone from having high anxiety and not being able to sleep the night before coming into the dental office, to actually looking forward to coming into the dentist, being excited to see who she's going to get for her hygienist or her assistant. Now she's preparing for braces and she's excited to get her braces on. The first time she came in to actually get her teeth pulled, as a dad, being the tough guy with his daughter, sitting here watching her getting her teeth pulled and not squirm, not cry…. um….. it actually brought…. um…. a little bit of emotion out when she was able to get it done without the fear or emotion or anxiety that comes with it. So having your daughter with that kind of calm and being able to go through that without being absolutely tormented or tortured is one of the best experiences a parent can have."

While one might argue that this gentleman might have not used terms like "tormented or tortured," the message he conveyed was clear. Having watched the video several times, I want to emphasize that where I wrote the two "ums," the man's wheels were obviously turning in his head as he wondered whether or not it would be all right to make an emotional state-ment. It was classically male. It was also marvelously touching to come from a man who may well have been a football player in his younger days, a self-described "tough guy." Outpourings like his were usually limited to the mothers of my practice. As a man myself, I am abundantly aware of the depth of feelings I have for my own children and the gratitude I feel for those who care for them. While I appreciate each accolade that is given to my work, it is special to receive it from another man. Unlike Randi's father, the firefighter, who possessed an economy of words, Tanya's father was willing to spell it out.

From my perspective, Tanya's experience was no great feat. Much of the art of being a dentist for children is to appreciate their sensitivities and to find a way of navigating around or through them. When I told Tanya that I was going to break a rule, I truly meant it. I did break a rule. When she asked me, "You'd do that for me?" I knew that being a rule-breaker would be just fine. Apparently, the tough guy also knew it would fine to break one of those unwritten rules of manhood. If rules are made to be broken, this was apparently the perfect time for both of us.

CHAPTER 10

Command performances

Some practice issues were harder to handle than others. If I saw a cavity in a tooth and the parent could see it, too, the decision to fill was simple. When I saw a child whose teeth were crooked and the parent could see it, too, the decision to pursue orthodontics was also easy. However, when I saw the results of a child's thumb sucking, things got more complicated. My discussion about the differences between mothers and fathers included how they dealt with the use of a pacifier. In many ways, the same could be said about thumb-sucking. This dichotomy expressed itself from the maternal side through explanations of how the habit was soothing for a child. Rarely did father make the same argument. Mothers would sometimes tell me that they had used socks on the children's hands, tape, cayenne pepper and multiple solutions to end the habit. Few succeeded. Others were simply not concerned about it. When I explained my concern about the possibility of a finger-sucking habit affecting a change in the child's bite, however, the parents' willingness to step in became greater.

For several years I used a product called Stop-zit for my thumb-sucking patients. It was an over-the-counter product that came in a small brown bottle with a twist-off cap that included a small brush to apply the material on the offending digits. My best description of this was that it smelled like, looked like, dried like, and, essentially in every way seemed like clear nail polish. When painted on a child's finger it was offensive to taste, which was the basis of using it to encourage children to stop sucking. At some point I was informed that the product was no longer available and was not being manufactured. I have no official information about why this happened, although I have often assumed that it may have been because the material was, in fact, clear nail polish and wasn't appropriate to put into a child's mouth.

I needed a new product. Fortunately, a wonderful compounding pharmacist in Olympia, Sandy, had come to my rescue at times of other needs, so I called him up. I explained that I needed a bio-safe product that would deter children from sucking on their fingers, and he said it would be no problem. He would incorporate a bio-safe astringent into a paste that would do the trick. He asked me what I wanted to call it. I hadn't considered that, so I told him I'd give him a call when I came up with something. Shortly after that, I called Sandy and told him I had the name. "What will you call it?" Sandy asked. I replied, "I want to call it Suck-cess." It, along with an entire behavior modification program I created, became the basis for my finger-sucking program, and it worked rather well. It wasn't 100% successful, but it had a high rate of success. The program was largely based on the child becoming aware of an unconscious habit, keeping track of when it happened and didn't happen, and then having the experience of stopping it. It was never the Suck-cess that did it. Only a person can stop a habit. The pills and products that are touted to be miracle cures are only tricks. In the end, a person must make that difficult choice to behave in a new way. It always delighted me when a child was successful, since I felt that she/he probably took heat at home about the habit. I could identify.

When I was a young child, I sucked on my middle and ring finger of my left hand. I don't know why, although I have seen incredible pictures of children sucking on fingers in utero. It might have just been the way it was. In the 1950's, it was not usual to ask your mother if you had been breast fed or had a bottle. Whichever it was, I was too young to remember and now I'm too old to remember. What I can clearly recall was my two older brothers pantomiming me with ludicrous facial expressions to accentuate their torment of me when they saw me with my fingers in my mouth. I suppose I felt some shame, but that didn't' stop me for quite a while. The date and reason for my stopping the habit are both long past and not a part of my knowledge base, but somehow, I did manage to keep my fingers out of my mouth. Whether it was the cause or not of the orthodontic care I later needed I cannot say. Based on my knowledge of the dynamics of the pressure from sucking on fingers, the forces exerted were, in their own fashion, orthodontic appliances. So, I would have to say that yes, my sixteen months in braces were most likely the result of my earlier oral obsession with my two fingers. A case study of one person does not warrant a scientific conclusion, but as I look back and see pictures of myself as a youngster, the migration of my two front teeth toward my nostrils is quite hard to miss.

Some of the children who underwent my Suck-cess program took the time to write me a note. Actually, it appears from the handwriting that it was the stenographer parent who wrote the note followed by the more age-appropriate autograph of the child. I always appreciated these tokens of acknowledgement. If my own actions had helped children such as Laura to keep her upper incisors inside her lip and under her nose, as opposed to looking a bit like Bugs Bunny, I was gratified. It was good to know that I held sway over some children when parents couldn't achieve the same result. When parents expressed their amazement at the dental treatment we could provide, I would point out that the advantage I had was not being the parent. Most parents understood this immediately.

Not every former finger-sucker was so artistic. Actually, many of them preferred not to even discuss their habit because of the negative feedback they had gotten at home. Even with the climactic and notable cessation of it, they would remain wordless. Not every one of them was lucky enough to keep their thoughts to themselves. Well-intentioned, but overzealous, parents (usually mothers) would step into the treatment area with enthusiastic admonitions to their children to "tell the doctor what you did." Never once did I assume it was something bad, because then it would be a matter for a confessional. Since many of the children being coaxed toward storytelling were usually in the three-four-five-year age group, I also didn't expect that they had become engaged. I knew exactly what the big achievement was because during our daily morning huddle, each child who was scheduled for the day would be reviewed so that I was aware that little Ashley had been given the Suck-cess program. One can only draw certain conclusions. Although mildly embarrassed for the child, I would play along and encourage the poor kid to tell me what had happened that had her mother so excited. After a few agonizing moments the child, squirming with discomfort, would say, "I quit sucking my finger." Now emoting myself, I would do my best characterization of an astonished person, verbally applauding the achievement. I would also promise two prizes for the day instead of the usual single one. Once things calmed down from these dramatic scenes, I would do my best to ask the child how she felt about it all. This was far more important to me, since I always believe that children should have their own moment of gaining esteem for an accomplishment rather than being drowned in phony accolades about how fabulous they were for everything they did. At times the child would respond with a smile. All I wanted was for that child to feel the success of the effort.

I played the violin when I was a kid. Well, let's just say I owned a violin and made some half-hearted attempts at playing it. When my two older brothers failed to take up a musical instrument, I believe my parents, recognizing I was their last chance to have a musical talent in the family, encouraged me to play the instrument. Unless my memory has failed me, I don't recall having pined to pick up this stringed instrument and painstakingly learn how to play it so that the songs were recognizable. I do recall the name Jascha Heifetz being mentioned frequently. Apparently, he was the reigning virtuoso on the violin during my childhood years. Being familiar with his name was the only thing I had in common with him.

My violin teacher at Lincoln School was a man who I retrospectively realized was of Russian origin. His name gave it away once I became aware of ethnicities. Richard Ivanovich had a shock of blond hair, sky-blue eyes, and a thin nose. He also had a manner about him that was so intimidating that I still wince a bit thinking about him. To his credit, he undoubtedly wanted his elementary school students to become actual musicians and did not hold back in his criticism when we were unprepared for the lessons. Sadly, that often described me. Much like my finger-sucking habit, my brothers were less than supportive of my woeful screeching on the strings of my violin. They would clamp their hands over their ears and run the other way. It wasn't a perfect environment for practicing. I felt intimidated and often wondered how and why I had managed to get myself into this predicament. I tried. I really did. I just didn't try often enough to be skilled with the instrument, and Mr. Ivanovich was quick to point that out in the clearest of terms. I believe the lessons were about twenty minutes each and rarely in my life have so few minutes lasted for such a long time. It was, however, a good lesson in life. Unless one is somehow born with an innate skill, talented people we admire reached their level with practice and very hard work. Musicians, athletes, actors, scientists, and authors did not exit the womb with their level of talent innately. That's why we admire them. When the school orchestra was assembled, I was assigned to the back row of the second violins. This was much like being the right fielder in Little League. I was happy to be hidden in the back of the orchestra where neither the audience nor Mr. Ivanovich would see me. The thought of performing a solo in front of anybody was mortifying to me.

I bless parents. I believe that every parent gets the right child. Just ask them. Not only very bright or gifted, there were parents who evaluated their children's talents in a rather subjective fashion. So it was with Amanda. This was a personable, rather quiet girl who had impeccable oral hygiene, an enthusiastic mother and, unbeknownst to me, her own Mr. Ivanovich. Living in Olympia, I occasionally saw in our local newspaper a story about one of my patients, and I would cut it out, include it with a note that I would hand write and send it to the youngster. It wasn't common to read about a patient who was younger than high school age, so, in truth, most of my patients had lives entirely unknown to me. I never knew if they played soccer, sang in a choir, wove baskets, or anything else. Some would share their exploits with me, but not the majority. Many times, the only way I found out was when the parents, much like the former finger suckers' parents, would present their children with a request, if not demand, if not ultimatum, to perform for me. This was Amanda's fate one day.

As she entered the treatment area, I noticed that she was carrying a case that either had a violin or a machine gun. Unlike the current mania for mass shooting, the latter idea never crossed my mind for a second. I was curious, though, about why she would bring a violin into the office for a dental visit. It took little time following the fluoride application to find out. Once I pronounced Amanda to again be in excellent dental health, her mother told me that her daughter had taken up the violin and was apparently a budding Jascha Heifetz. Always quick to pick up on any scrap of information and turn it into a conversation, I mentioned that I had played the violin as a child. To that, Amanda's mother told me that in that case, I would be certain to enjoy hearing Amanda play a bit. This is never an easy situation to escape gracefully, so I concurred. Out came the violin. Out came the bow. Amanda put rosin on the bow and struck the classic violinist position. All of this, of course, was happening in the treatment room. I admired her pluck and wondered which Mozart opera overture or Beethoven concert piece she may have prepared for me. Amanda dug into the strings with the bow and out flowed a nearly flawless rendition of "Twinkle, Twinkle, Little Star." I had to hand it to her. She played it very well. And then she played it again. And again. And again. I'd guess it was about eight to ten times so that now I was concerned about delaying my entire schedule while listening to this little personal concert. Her mother smiled that proud smile that only a parent can invoke, and Amanda continued sawing away when I finally had to excuse myself to see another patient. She was the only musical performer in my career and, like other children who had command performances, it was memorable enough immortalize it in my book.

Twinkle, twinkle, little star

Chapter 11

The times when magic happened

There was a time when magic happened. When the Polaroid camera first came out, it was a sensation that a picture could be developed right before your eyes. I have never understood the technology (or chemistry) behind this, but I remember thinking, "This is magic." I was, of course, rather young, which undoubtedly led me to my conclusion. Regardless, the mere idea that it was possible to hold an actual photograph within seconds, without taking it to a camera store or sending it to a laboratory, was fantastic. What's more, it was a tactile experience. Aim, fire, wait a few moments and the blank object in your hand became a photograph. It was amazing and it was magic.

Today we live in the digital world. I read recently that the iPhone, iPad and iPod are aptly named since they all start with "i." This could be considered one of the hallmarks of the 21st century. It's all about "I," or to make that grammatically correct, it's all about *me*. A part of me mourns the loss of direct interpersonal contact. I am at a loss at a restaurant when a couple, young or old, sits across from each other staring at their respective cell phones. To the best of my knowledge, there is not yet a twelve-step program to break the addiction to cell phones. We have all seen people walking down busy sidewalks with their eyes glued to their phones. Worse yet, we have read about traffic accidents that were caused by the driver texting while driving. I have heard that the people who are most convinced that they can "multi-task" are usually the ones least capable of doing it. However, this new world is also magic. I grew up at a time when Dick Tracy's wrist radio was considered science fiction. I attended college at a time when computer science, or "comp sci," was taught with punch cards. Students would have a stack of cards about four inches tall, and, if an error was made on a single card, the program would not run. Now, we essentially carry computers around in our pockets or purses. They are called cell phones. They, like the Polaroid camera in its day, are magic.

In these devices, pictures also appear in a second, but they are not held in one's hand. They are enshrined in a camera among thousands of others that are likewise stored there. We pass our cell phones back and forth to show off our grandchildren, our pets, our gardens, or our latest trip. Nobody walks away with those pictures. They live in the phone.

When I think back on the many ways things have changed, I become more nostalgic than upset. This is a soliloquy to the past when things moved more slowly, and our hands were more "on" than not. Since dentistry required that my hands were literally on my patients, I spent many years in that mode. Maybe that's why I miss it. To begin a dental appointment with a child by diving into his/her mouth was never an appropriate starting point. With parental admonitions "not to talk to strangers," children must have had those words ringing in their ears when they entered a space with strange equipment and masked people dressed in strange clothes saying strange things. No wonder some of them opted to keep their mouths shut. Some children were armed and loaded for conversation while others were beyond reticent. They were mute.

One of our strategies to begin our relationship with our patients was to take their picture each time they had a cleaning appointment with us. That typically meant every six months. It was a familiar activity that also allowed us to easily segue into "taking pictures of your teeth," which would introduce the children to another strange apparatus and a mildly irritating object placed inside their mouths. I liked that the great majority of children had already been well coached in the "smile for the camera" mantra.

Their first moments at each visit were marked by smiling, having a picture taken, and then off to the job at hand. We would write the child's first name on the front, last name on the back, and often included a smiley face next to the name. We could do all this because for the first several years in the practice, the pictures were taken with a Polaroid camera. That, by itself, was part of the magic. The picture was taken, and the photo would pop out of the camera. Initially it was blank, but within moments the image would begin to materialize in front of the child's own eyes. Many times, those same eyes would enlarge at this magical process. And it was tactile. They held the picture in their hands. It wasn't necessary to page through the 10,000 photos stored on a phone to find the child's face. It was the one-and-only picture. Even better was the fact that it would become the child's own possession when she/he returned in six months. We always kept the most recent one and gave the previous photo to the child. Or so we thought. It was the *parents* who loved these things. Some asked us to always take the picture in the exact same place so that a comparison of the child's growth could be determined.

The Polaroids were popular beyond my expectations and, to a degree, beyond my understanding. Most important to me, though, was that they served a strategic purpose in the management of my patients. They also created problems. We had solved the film issue by purchasing cases of film from Costco and we never ran out. When taking thirty or more pictures each day, we quickly used entire ten-packs, but never ran out. However, as with all pieces of equipment, the cameras ultimately stopped working. They failed to announce their pending demise, though, so it would always come as a surprise on a random day. An assistant would nervously approach me and tell me that the camera wasn't working. I'd check the batteries and any other potential problem areas and, if I couldn't find anything to fix, I knew its days were over. The first time this occurred, I discovered how important these pictures were. Parents wanted to know where their children's pictures were! I was certain that I ran a dental practice, not a photo studio, but the obvious disappointment on the faces of the parents taught me that this little management trick we used for the benefit of the children was actually something that the parents also loved.

When I was a child, my father assembled photo albums for my brothers and me so that I have a pictorial record of much of my life. This became something that I also did for my own children.... or anyway, up until the advent of digital photography. Now those albums are called cell phones or computer files. My daughter, in particular, loved to peruse her albums, especially with some of her boyfriends. It was tactile. Apparently not every parent had the same idea, so the Polaroids from my office were possibly the only pictorial history they possessed of their sons' or daughters' childhoods. Realizing how special the photos were, I bought a second Polaroid camera so that we would always have a spare when one came to its final moment.

Much like running into parents who would remind me that "I was their children's dentist," I also discovered that the Polaroids were often among the desk decorations for many of them. It might be at an attorney's office, my CPA's receptionist, or a nurse at a medical facility. There they stood with a patient's smile beaming out of the picture along with the smiley face and name on the front. Luckily for me, with a quick glance I could "remember" the name of the person's child, ask how "Mandy" was doing, and receive in return a smile and a grateful look. I didn't promote my practice every moment, but I never stopped remembering that for any given adult, that child was at the top of a list of love. It was satisfying that the Polaroid pictures from my practice gave them that brief moment to look at their children's faces.

Sadly, the Polaroid cameras and film disappeared, still another relic of yesteryear. From the viewpoint of a modernizing traditionalist, few things that were so basic served in so many ways. I liked those pictures myself. I still have some of my own children, since they, too, were patients in my practice. With all the complex modern gadgets we now consider routine, it is with fondness that I think back on the Polaroids and know that it was often the simple things that made life special. Some of them were even magic.

SECTION 5- SPEAKING AND BRINGING STORIES TO LIFE

They pay you to talk?

I still recall sitting in my living room as our practice's facilitator, during one of our out-of-the-office planning sessions, asked everyone to tell the group the biggest idea they had for the future. The germ of the idea had been planted during my residency and then temporarily bloomed during my time with the Navy. Since then, it had merely sat dormant in the back of my mind. It was a big vision and one that I felt I could not only handle, but do very well. Then there was the little devil sitting on my shoulder asking me just who I thought I was to believe that I could do such a thing. Up until this meeting, that little devil had always won the day. Since I heard some of my team members expressing their hopes and dreams for their own future, I was struck by their courage and inspired by their words. The practice had often felt very much like family to me since we spent as much (or more) time together than we did with our own families for most of the week. It was this perfect blend of factors that gave me the strength.

"I want to be a national speaker on the dental continuing education circuit," I stated. The silence that met my announcement only fanned the flames of that doubt. I did not see one person nodding her head with eager agreement. My imagination told me that they were thinking exactly what I had long thought—just who is this guy to go out and teach others about pediatric dentistry? Finally, Jeanne, our brilliant facilitator, said words that she often brought to conversations. She simply uttered, "Tell me more." With that I began to relate my history of presenting courses in the Navy and, somewhat to my surprise, nobody on the Team had even known this about me. My enthusiasm grew as I related how the dentists in my audiences not only lacked a depth of knowledge about caring for children, but they also actually knew far less than I did.

Encouraged by Jeanne's positive response as well as the Team's increasing curiosity about what I had done, I finally let myself begin to make my dream come true. I had no idea what that would entail, but I now have spoken at about three hundred dental meetings and delivered almost a thousand lectures in thirty-five states and six foreign countries. I can look back on that moment in the Team meeting that tipped the balance toward one of the most rewarding professional endeavors I have experienced. My father always told me that I had the blood of Demosthenes, the famous Greek orator, running through my veins, but I doubt even he could have imagined me standing in front of crowds of people who paid attention to me for three hours at a time. I, myself, had to occasionally marvel at the thought that people paid me to talk.

CHAPTER 1

Big things happen in small towns

During my years in the navy, I had taken literally hundreds of clinical photographs. These are not pictures one would show to neighbors, as they generally were dominated by molars, tongues, and other oral structures. Many were pictures of severely decayed teeth, which, when shown to a lay person, would always bring a gasp of astonishment that such a thing could exist. They would often ask, "Do you see that often?" I would answer, "Just about every day." Armed with my vast library of Kodachrome slides, all organized into carousels, I prepared several talks about the many aspects of my specialty and felt ready to market myself. The trouble was, I had no idea how to do that. There were no personal computers then, no internet, and no Facebook. I did, however, have a directory from the state dental association that included the names of all the directors of the state dental meetings, and, with that information, I began to send out letters and information about my material. I was confident my mailbox would be filled with offers. In fact, there was not a single one. I persisted for quite a while, holding out hope that if I could just get that one invitation, the rest would come pouring in. That was not the case.

One of the aspects of being a specialist is that local dental societies are eager to provide continuing education to their members and they often ask specialists to come to a meeting to do a 30-minute presentation. Since I already had my carousels loaded with my slides, this was an easy task. It also provided more exposure to any of the outlying dentists who had not met me. Not only would I bring a lecture to my own dental society, but other groups to the north, south and west would invite me to speak. I always felt that it gave me the opportunity to polish my material for when the big invitation would arrive. I did quite a bit of polishing, but still, I heard nothing from any of the directors.

The mother of one of my patients was an instructor at a dental hygiene school north of Olympia. She casually asked me one day if I would consider coming to her school and speak to the second-year students about behavior management of the child patient. It thrilled me to get this invitation, but, ironically, it was the one topic for which I had not prepared a lecture. Nevertheless, I told Kaitlin that I'd be more than happy to do that. As became more the norm than the exception, when invited to do a presentation, it was the invitation itself that started my creativity to develop a cogent presentation. In this case, I had no idea at the time that I was about to develop one of the most popular, most requested, and most appreciated lectures of my entire series of presentations.

Initially my talk about behavior management focused more on the technical aspects of the skill set. Emphasis was placed on terminology, and I invented an exercise during which audience members would come up to the front of the room in groups. I would then explain that I was about to give them a command that I used in my practice every day, and, as soon as an individual responded appropriately, I would have that person return to her seat. Each command was simple. I told them to hold still, put your hands on your stomach, and smile for me. The "trick" to the exercise was that I asked each of these simple commands in a different foreign language. My travels had come in handy so that I could ask them in Greek, German, and Japanese. I would also make sure that some of them "got it" by varying my approach from repetitive monotone to yelling at them to showing them with my hands what I wanted them to do. I then explained that we in dentistry have our own foreign language so that we have to make certain that the children could understand what was being asked of them. Of course, other aspects of behavior management were included, but it was the terminology section that was always the most profound, simply because the attendees were forced to stand in the shoes of their patients. It was a lesson in reality rather than in theory.

Kaitlin reported to me that the lecture was very popular, and it became an annual event. When the other instructors began attending the classes and also gave it high marks, Kaitlin told me she felt she could get me a slot at the state dental hygiene conference, which became my first paid presentation. In May, 1995, I spoke at that meeting in Everett, Washington. With my two carousels and more evaluation forms than necessary, I launched my new career before a crowd of perhaps eighty hygienists. Both exhilarated and exhausted afterwards, I had still another push-pull about whether this was a good idea or not. The preparation time for the lectures was more than I had anticipated, especially when a topic was requested for which I had not prepared material. The effort was significant to sort slides and put them into two carousels to ensure that all would be smooth with the double-projector presentations. Still, my motivation hadn't waned, and I persisted. Over the next four years I spoke at ten other meetings. Most of them were dental hygiene groups, as the network of instructors told those at other schools about me. I also spoke at the national Dental Hygiene Conference in San Diego, California, which was my first national exposure. I was beginning to enjoy it, but I still wanted to catch on to the much larger dental conferences. It was four years into the process, and I still had a total of zero invitations for a major dental meeting.

Eventually, I learned why my self-promotion was futile. Once I was established as a speaker on the continuing education circuit, the directors of the various conferences told me that they are inundated by requests to speak and generally don't even open the packets that are sent to them. I was initially peeved, but I have come to understand their point. The usual rule for a speaker to be invited to a given meeting is that she/he must have been heard by a member of that meeting's continuing education committee. Having attended many dental conferences myself, I was oblivious to the other world that was happening at them. Depending on the size of the conference, scouts from other meetings would come into the lecture halls to determine if a speaker was able to present in a coherent fashion, keep the audience engaged, and fit the material into the assigned time frame. This all makes sense to me now, but as with other aspects of life, when you aren't aware of the way things are, you are shooting in the dark. That was certainly the case for me. You may wonder, then, who it was that heard me speak that netted my first *dental conference* invitation.

My referral base, as I have previously described, covered a large area because of the geographic location of Olympia. For the first five or six years of my practice, there was only one other pediatric dentist in town, and he had less interest in providing programs for the outlying dental societies. When a third pediatric dentist came to town, he was also not so interested. Given my drive to establish myself as a speaker, it was relatively easy to attract invitations from the local dental societies. One of these dental societies is located on the Pacific coastline, due west of Olympia. The town, Aberdeen, had several dentists and at least three or four of them were excellent referral sources for my practice. I never knew to whom the dentists referred their pediatric patients, but I was aware of the ones who sent children to me for care. When I was asked to speak at a December meeting in 1998, I accepted without hesitation even though this coincided with the time when I was on the brink of giving up my efforts to become a national speaker. I packed up my two Kodak projectors, extension cords, screen, carousels, and started driving out Highway 101 from Olympia. Since it was December and I set out at about 4:30, it was already dark, and it was raining. There was no GPS, and I was driving alone, so finding the restaurant where the meeting was being held was the first challenge. In fact, I drove right past it and, finally realizing that I must have gone too far, did a U-turn and then found it after backtracking about two miles. The meeting wasn't due to start until 6:00, so I had plenty of time to get my gear out, set it all up, and do a quick dry run of my 30-minute talk on primary tooth pulp therapy. Then I settled into my chair to await the crowd.

Shortly before 6:00, dentists began to trickle in, and the flow never exceeded a trickle. When the meeting was called to order, attendance figures came in at six. I do my best to always be as professional as possible, but I admit to having thoughts run through my mind that sounded something like "drive for an hour through rain, miss the restaurant, get here early to set up, and a whopping six people show up. Why, exactly, am I doing this?" In spite of my internal monolog, I proceeded to give the "crowd" my best, which has always been my mantra. Since my talk was the finale of the meeting, as soon as the words, "Any questions?" came out of my mouth, people began filing out at a pace faster than they had come into the room. None of this was uplifting to me, but I always felt it went with the territory. If I successfully instructed them to do the procedures properly or if I influenced one of the attendees toward referring patients to me, I decided to be satisfied with that. Within ten minutes, each of them would be back in his home while I would still be packing up my equipment.

"Very nice presentation"

When I gathered all my things to take out to my car, one of the attendees returned to the room. "Very nice presentation," he said. I thanked him and then, much like Stan McAndrew's suggestion that I look into Dr. Stock's project, this person changed my life in a minute. He didn't know that I was momentarily down and seriously thinking of simply ending my dreams of speaking at dental meetings. "You should be on the state dental meeting program," he stated. I thanked him again but explained that I had been trying for years to get an invitation, but that I now understood that to do so required that a scout from that state dental association needed to have heard me speak to warrant it. "I'm Tom Waterton," he continued, "and I'm the president of the Washington State Dental Association this year. If you call Ruth at the WSDA office tomorrow, tell her that I want you on the program." I recognized Ruth's name as the executive director of the dental conference for the Washington State Dental Association. Slightly stunned, I had far less problem acting on Tom's words than I did when Stan told me about Dr. Stock's project. If Tom were to be my ticket to a dental conference, I was ready to make that call. I did wait until about 8:01 the next morning. When I reached the receptionist, I asked her to put me in touch with Ruth, expecting to be questioned why. No questions were asked and a brief moment later I was in direct contact with the woman who had the power to add me to the state's dental meeting. I explained the entire situation and Ruth's response was, "If Dr. Waterton wants you for the meeting, you're on the program."

Yogi Berra had it right when he said, "It ain't over 'til it's over." Two important lessons in my life were delivered by entirely unlikely sources. On the brink of quitting dental school, I was guided into the specialty that I have loved for forty-six years. At the moment I thought of quitting my pursuit of a career as a speaker at dental conferences, a member of my smallest crowd (ever!) stepped up and gave me the pathway to another delight of my life. I don't necessarily believe in coincidences, but I definitely believe that keeping my eyes, ears, and mind open to anything can lead to something greater than I might have imagined.

CHAPTER 2

The ups and downs, the smiles and frowns

Even though I was well prepared, I was still a bit nervous as my first ever dental conference crowd filed into the diminutive room I was assigned. As I pondered this first step, I was happy to recall my father's words of many years prior. When my dad told me, "You have the blood of Demosthenes flowing through your veins" I didn't know who Demosthenes was. When I discovered he was the orator who practiced speaking with a mouthful of stones, it didn't seem like the best way to launch my new career, especially since I am a dentist. I was still outfitted with my projectors and the carousels filled with my slides. I had prepared as best I could to deliver a lengthier version of the behavior management lecture I had done for the dental hygiene schools. Since I was a first-time speaker, the capacity of the room was about sixty, but to me it wasn't the size of the crowd that was important. I had arrived. My foot was in the door, and as long as I could deliver, my nearly abandoned dream might return to life.

Many dental lectures are, quite frankly, very dull. Others are irrelevant to my own professional education. There are endless scientific facts in some, microscopic views of cells, proportions of mixing materials and other details that don't always make for scintillating moments. Other presentations include pictures of hideous looking mouths that have been restored gorgeously. My own experience was that many of the procedures being shown were so far beyond my own ability that I couldn't help wondering if the entire point of the presentation was self-aggrandization. My goal was to make sure that everything I brought out in my talk could be done by anyone in my audience. I also included stories, such as the ones I have included in this book. They usually got good laughs and sometimes got tears of empathy. I wanted my lectures to be different than the norm because I figured a sleeping audience would not learn much.

I had listened to another pediatric dentist speak at a meeting in Vancouver, British Columbia, and I learned two things. The first thing I learned was that it was possible to have a lecture that was fun. He was engaging, humorous, and very lively. He didn't stand behind the podium and drone for hours. He came out into the audience to give a more personal feel to his talk. I liked his presentation and realized that a continuing education course needn't be dry or boring. With that realization, I felt it would be possible to add funny stories about my experiences without diminishing the value of the overall lecture. After all, I wasn't a stand-up comedian. I was a professional speaker who was there to educate the attendees, but I was convinced that a blend of education and entertainment would create the best experience for those who were listening.

The second thing I learned at the Vancouver meeting was that my specialty needed a different banner carrier than the man whom I heard. He had been the pediatric dental headliner for quite a while and was popular in spite of the philosophy he advocated. As with all things in the world, pediatric dentistry is constantly evolving. The approach professed by the speaker that day was so far from what I felt the majority of my peers were doing that I wanted to provide a different vision. The techniques the speaker described were all familiar to me, but I had moved far past them and now considered them to be somewhat archaic. The experience was critical to my planning and my execution of the lecture at the Washington State Dental Meeting in Seattle on July 15, 1999.

When the first hearty laugh came out of the audience, I knew things would be fine. Sensing that my combination of facts, techniques, stories, and humor was a good blend, and that people were engaged, I was invigorated.

Even during that first talk, I loosened up my own presentation style and received the response I wanted. I was on my way. Slightly disturbing were the people who would come into the lecture hall with a clipboard. They would only stay for about five minutes or so and disappear. At this early stage of my speaking career, I had no idea that scouts from other meetings were always checking on speakers they hadn't yet heard in order to bring new educators to their own conferences. Flushed with what I considered the success of my first dental conference performance, I was putting all my gear away when a man approached me. He introduced himself as Brandon Woods and asked if I'd like to speak at that same Vancouver, British Columbia meeting where I had decided to become an alternative speaker for my specialty. It was difficult to withhold my enthusiasm, but I told him it would be my honor to do so. He took my card and said he would contact me with more details. When I didn't hear from him for quite a while, my hopes dropped again, but only with time did I come to realize that most major dental conferences book speakers two years in advance. Another man came into my room and complimented me on my lecture and told me he was a scout for the American Dental Association Meeting, probably the biggest meeting in the country. He invited me as well. Both invitations came through for the respective 2001 meetings. A great number of scouts were at the ADA Meeting and, from that moment, my speaking dream became a reality.

My speaking has taken me many places in the United States, as well as Canada, Germany, Russia, Mexico, Kuwait, and Australia. When I began, my stated goal was to educate and to have people pay for my travels. Little did I know what a small vision that was. Much like the choice of my career has brought me an abundance of surprises, pleasures, and rewards, the same can be said for my career as a dental educator. I now belong to a fraternity (and sorority) of people who are dedicated to helping others be better dentists, hygienists, and assistants. I have friends from all over and have spoken at several meetings multiple times. I sometimes laugh about the fact that I see some of my speaking friends more often that I see my own children. It's not that I fail to see my kids, it's that I might have up to fifteen engagements per year that would take me to Chicago, Atlanta, San Antonio, or Anaheim, and when at each one, I would again see my fellow speakers who were from Toronto, Greensboro, Los Angeles, Richmond, Dallas, San Francisco, and many other places. It became a social outlet for me as well. It also demanded that I stay on top of my material so that I didn't become the next out-of-date speaker, talking about things that were long since abandoned.

I must add, though, that it also brought out a part of me that had lain rather dormant for most of my life. My oldest brother was always the life of the party sort of person, and when he and I were at a given place at the same time, I couldn't get in a word edgewise. People thought he was hilarious, and it was clear that I couldn't compete with him for people's attention or laughs. As my lectures continued to develop, I kept adding more and more stories as well as role-plays in which I would play the part of the worried mother, the happy child, or the angry father, just to name a few. My will-ingness to let myself go for the benefit of the audience grew with time. I was enjoying myself while educating, and, from most of the feedback I received, they were having fun while learning. It was not unusual to get a comment such as, "this was the first lecture that I stayed awake the entire time." My thespian skills improved, and the popularity grew.

It wasn't all positive, though. At each lecture the audience was asked to fill out an evaluation form. I always read them. Clearly there were some who were less pleased with my material, but fortunately that tended to be the exception rather than the rule. Typically, the rating scale would be the traditional 1 to 5 with "excellent" being the 5. In most cases for every one hundred evaluations I would receive, there would be seventy-five 5's, twen-ty-four 4's and one 1. Initially I would fret about the person who would give me a 1, which indicated "poor." I would search through the comments sec-tion for a clue about what that individual may have wanted or disliked, but there would usually be no clue about why I had received such a low mark. In order to find a graceful and psychologically tolerable way to deal with this, I decided that that person who gave me the 1 must simply be dyslexic. She/he probably thought my lecture was fine, but just marked the wrong end of the scale. Whether or not that was true has never bothered me. It has certainly helped deal with that little stab of rejection that I might have felt. Regardless, my career in front of crowds brought out a part of me that

I'm not sure I even knew existed. Moscow, Russia, and Hobart, Tasmania, were far cries from my dark, rainy night in Aberdeen, Washington. I'm grateful that I stuck with it. It became yet another blessing in my life and when my stories came to life, I realized that that common human thread that runs through all of us just might result in an entertaining and educational memoir.

Chapter 3

Feedback and impact

My goal in speaking was to educate dental professionals about how to better care for children. I did this by simply telling people what I did and the results I got. I always knew that my style would not work for each attendee at my lectures. In part I knew this intuitively and, in part I learned it from the course evaluations that were always made available to me. Fortunately, there were not often negative comments or dissatisfied audience members. I did find it disappointing that some people had spent three hours listening to me and felt that nothing had been gained. Any sense of failure I may have carried, however, was always balanced by the many positive comments I received as well as the impact I had in career choices of people who had heard me speak or came to my office to observe. The following are merely a small sampling.

From an anonymous attendee at a meeting at the California Dental Association meeting in Anaheim, California (and I quote):

> "This is the second time I am attending a lecture you are presenting. Before the first presentation years ago, I was an assistant who avoided child appointments at all costs. I was in fear of scaring them trying to get them to comply, keeping

them still for treatment and the BIGGY, I was afraid I would make them cry, signaling 'parent bears' to come rushing in for the rescue.

After the first lecture of yours, I went back to the office and just couldn't wait for the next child appointment. I downloaded the parent information for pre-visit/treatment. The first child visit went without any negative incidents. And it has been like that ever since.

I look forward to children now in the office. The dentist was so impressed with my new skills. I think even he was calmer. I had many parents thank and compliment me, but it was all due to the lecture I attended that your presented.

Thank you, from Me

P.S. You don't practice in California, but you are helping so many in So. Cal through me."

Several years ago, I received a call from John, my wife's dentist, and a man I had known for many years as an excellent general dentist in the Olympia area. He asked if his daughter, who was interested in becoming a dental hygienist, could shadow me in my office. He wanted her to see another way that hygienists, at least in Washington State, could provide care. I have had many students come into my practice to shadow me or my hygienist to experience how the "real world" would be if they pursued a career in dentistry. Not every single one turned out like this one, though. Alicia, John's daughter, came in to observe how my hygienist had opportunities to do so much more than simply clean teeth all day. She was attentive, asked many appropriate questions, and stayed the entire day, which was unusual. Many others who shadowed would whistle-stop through a morning in order to write on an application that they had observed in a dental practice, which had led to a great desire to become a dentist or a hygienist. In Alicia's case, she did not bolt after the morning and seemed to be shadowing *me* as much as she was shadowing Diana, my hygienist. At the end of the day, she thanked us for the opportunity to come into the practice and discover what the future might hold for her.

Not having heard anything from either Alicia or her father, I phoned John to find out if his daughter had enjoyed her experience and if she was more prepared to apply for hygiene school. John was not the most talkative man I had ever met, so his response was rather brief, but very meaningful. He said, "No, she isn't planning to apply to hygiene school." I was surprised enough to become speechless. John continued, "She now wants to be a pediatric dentist." I was thrilled. The moment of clarity comes to each of us in its own way. For Alicia, it was the opportunity to witness the joy and satisfaction of being a dentist for children. She is now a pediatric dentist in Olympia and, several years later, I received a heart-warming card from her. On the outside cover it said:

"In life, there are many paths you take and many people who share the journey…"

Inside the card it continued: "But it's the special people who help you along the way, and it's the most important people who care enough to give of themselves unconditionally. Thank you for being one of those special people."

The personal, hand-written note that was inside the card read, "Dear Greg, I feel so blessed to have had the opportunity to shadow in your office and to get to know you. You have been such an important influence in my life. Thank you for sharing your passion for Pediatric Dentistry with me. I would not be where I am today without your guidance and mentorship. I love my career and I am forever grateful.

Many thanks, (Alicia)"

From an experienced pediatric dentist who attended a program at a major dental meeting:

"Dear Greg,

I was impressed with both of your presentations. Your delivery skill really helps people to enjoy the topic and LISTEN. Specifically, keep telling funny stories, using parent impersonations, and voice intonations. Your material is very timely and a good review, even for me. Scary, but even I learned some stuff.

Thanks, (Ronald Chance)"

I received a card from a dental assistant from Tucson, AZ following a presentation for the Pacific Coast Society of Orthodontics:

"Dear Dr. Psaltis,

Hello! I had the pleasure of attending your lecture at this year's PCSO in October in Seattle. I wanted to write you personally to tell you how much I enjoyed it! I laughed so much! It was by far the best lecture I have been to in my personal 16 years of orthodontic assisting. You will be pleased to know I came back home to Tucson, AZ that following Monday and utilized one of your techniques on a nine-year old boy. It worked! I specifically requested for my boss to allow me to go to your lecture to learn how to handle what we call TLC patients. So I wanted to send you a great big Thank You!

Sincerely, (Rhonda Salazar)"

While I do my best to both educate and entertain my audiences, it is particularly satisfying to receive an email, card or letter that informs me that my information has made life better for both patients and the professionals caring for them. Comments on the evaluation forms also indicated that the humor in my presentations not only keeps attendees alert and focused, but creates a shared experience, since nearly everyone in the room can identify with situations I have experienced.

For seven or eight years I lectured the third-year dental students at the University of Washington School of Dentistry in Seattle. I was specifically asked to present my concepts about dealing with parents, which is often problematic for many dental professionals. I was always struck with how young the students seemed to be. I also appreciated the enthusiasm they exuded during my talk. It was different than speaking at a dental conference because there was greater uniformity of the attendees in age. Also, the size of the group was small enough to see which of the students would never consider pediatric dentistry and which ones were intrigued. Following one of the lectures a woman approached me as I was putting my computer away. She told me that she loved the lecture and said that she was interested in the Cabo volunteer clinic that I ran. Experience has taught me that excitement runs high in that moment of hearing something new and stimulating. Countless people have told me they wanted to participate in the project right up until the time I needed volunteers to commit. Then they couldn't seem to work it out. I deal with this by telling individual to email me to indicate interest in writing so I can add her/him to my list. Such was the case with Priscilla. She wrote that evening, expressing the hope that she could join a group. Frankly I hadn't expected her to follow through since she was still a student, but I put her name on my list of candidates. It was about six months later that I was recruiting a team and, as I worked my way through my list, I continued to get negative responses for various reasons. Finally, the last person on the list was Priscilla. I remembered her and, with some doubt in my mind, wrote to her with the dates of my upcoming trip. It was about an hour later that she replied saying that she was eager to join me. I was impressed. That June my team of Priscilla, Joan and I became the last group to work at the Niños del Kapitan clinic in Cabo San Lucas. While tentative, Priscilla showed great interest in everything we were doing, and it may have been her experience of witnessing the magic that we worked on Magdalena (described in the introduction of this book) that convinced her that becoming a pediatric dentist was her goal. She completed her residency and is now a practicing specialist for children in Texas.

Following another of my talks at the UW School of Dentistry a young man approached me and asked if he could come to Olympia to observe my practice. As always, I gave him my contact information and told him when he was ready, he could come at any time. The practice never prepared a special day for the benefit of our guests. We simply had them walk into a day that had been scheduled prior to their request and find out, along with us, what it held. Not long after the day of the lecture, Luke contacted me, and we set a date for his visit. Like Alicia, he spent the entire day at the office. Before returning to Seattle, he told me that the experience convinced him to pursue pediatric dentistry. He, too, is now a dentist solely for children.

I have not actively tried to "sell" my specialty to anyone. I have merely told my stories, explained my techniques, and expressed my own enthusiasm. At times, they could witness those joys in my practice. My intent was never to recruit people into pediatric dentistry. As I look back, I seriously doubt that it was ever the fillings or fluoride applications that captured the hearts of the people who responded to my talks. It was always the personal relationship aspects of my work that gripped them. In some cases, it was enough to propel them into two or three more years of education in order to obtain their specialty training and certification. All of this is a celebration for the knowledge that telling people what I do has had a significant impact on others. It has reminded me that much like Stan McAndrew, Dr. Stock, Luz Cordero, and Tom Waterton, I have also been that key person who appeared in the lives of others at the right moment to change their futures. It was my speaking career that expanded my sphere of influence in many ways—from helping the attendees deal with children more effectively to inspiring young dentists to specialize. The situations presented here are only the ones about which I am specifically aware. In my mind's eye, I feel certain that there are others who were similarly affected. I just don't know about them. As with most parts of my life, while I strive to do my best, it is not my intention to have others be just like me. My wife kindly, but clearly, points out that just one of me is enough for the world. This is undoubtedly true.

SECTION 6- THE MEXICO PROJECTS

Coming full circle

It somehow only seems right that I would bookend my career in this way. I came full circle by wrapping up my career by founding two volunteer dental projects in Mexico. Back in the California Central Valley, Luz Cordero stole my heart and vaulted me into the direction that would bring me much satisfaction, joy, and fulfillment. She would not be the last Latina child to endear herself to me. Memories of Dr. Stock and his vision for caring for less fortunate youngsters coursed through my mind when I was first invited by a friend to join her in Zihuatanejo, Mexico. We were to work in the office of Doctora Valeria, providing the much needed and otherwise unavailable treatment for the children of the area. Much like my fateful moment with Luz, this experience provided the impetus to move in a specific new direction. I decided to form my own volunteer programs in Mexico. They are not identical to Dr. Stock's, except for the intention.

The project in Zihuatanejo has been a very personal one for me. Not only could I care for children, but I also became friends with Valeria, her family, and other dentists in the surrounding areas who would come to help on the project. It became the "connection" project since I spent so much time with local people both in and out of the dental setting. The rewards that came from it were much like any other volunteer work one might choose to do. However, in Zihua, as we came to call the city, it went far beyond that in so many ways. It would be difficult, if not impossible, to duplicate the atmosphere of that program since so much heart went into from so many people. It was also easier for me since the clinic was already in existence and Valeria would do all the prep work of finding the patients and arranging the appointments. I just had to show up. For me, it became more than a dental project because of the warmth and hospitality of Valeria, her family, and the people of the city. I take pride in the treatment we provided, but I also felt a sense of statesmanship by working, eating, and sometimes playing side by side with the wonderful Mexican people I met there.

Once I had tasted the sweetness of volunteer dentistry, I felt an instant rush that almost felt like an addiction. While it was very satisfying, spending one week per year with Dra. Valeria wasn't enough. Cabo San Lucas had been considered my family's Mexican home for several years, and I decided I wanted to bring my healing skills there as well. I asked some of my friends in the town about the possibility of volunteering there and whom I should contact to make it a reality. Ultimately, I met Gayle, the executive director of a non-profit in the city. The Amigos de los Niños was an organization that focused on the medical needs of children, particularly those with hearing loss, strabismus (crossed eyes), heart problems and cancer. It felt it was the right place to start. Along with Diana, the hygienist who had introduced me to Valeria, I traveled to Cabo to speak with Gayle. She listened intently to the plan without much response. When I finally asked her what she thought, she wordlessly stared at us. When I posed the question again, she simply said, "I don't see how this is going to work." I asked her for more information. "You want to see children who don't speak English, have never been to a dentist and, in many cases, have never seen a foreigner, and you want to provide dental work for them. Is that correct?" Gayle asked. "Yes," I replied. She repeated her skepticism, "I don't see how that is going to work." Many people cannot understand how any child can be the happy recipient of dental care, so this response did not surprise me. Undaunted, I suggested that she could find someone who would let us work for two mornings. If it didn't work out, I would never contact her again. She agreed to the plan, and it became the launch of my second Mexico project, which would not only provide me with a second reason to head to the Baja California sun, but it would also expand beyond my wildest dreams.

When people hear about the work I do in Mexico, they almost always tell me, "That is so wonderful that you do that." I wouldn't disagree, but as anyone who has ever volunteered time for the benefit of the less fortunate, the blessings go both ways. I tell those who compliment me on my efforts that while I am filling children's teeth, they are filling my heart. That is more than a bargain. It is a blessing. I'm sure Dr. Stock is smiling somewhere.

CHAPTER 1

If only all my patients could be like this

When the Zihua project began, it was a rather modest operation. Valeria's office had a single chair, and we would see about ten patients per day for four days. At times it felt as though we were throwing a pebble into a pond, but at least we were doing something. I wished there might be a way to treat more of these delightful children but rushing them through their visits just to see more of them made no sense. We were better with the pebble than with a gust of wind. At least we helped out some of them and we knew we'd be back the following year.

Bernardo when we first met him in 2005

We had "regulars" and one of them in particular captured our hearts. When Bernardo showed up at his first visit with us, he wore a white hat, blue shirt, gray vest, and a wonderful smile. He wasn't overly shy, but not overly talkative either. We connected, whether words were shared or not. How could we not with a boy in this outfit?

The youngest of several children, his parents abandoned him and his siblings, most of whom went to live with one set of grandparents. They didn't quite have enough space for all the children, so Bernardo was sent to the home of his other grandfather. Each year both of them would appear for dental care, and each year we relished the thought of seeing them again. Lucky for us, Bernardo wore the same hat several times so that his growth could be calibrated not by marks on a wall, but by how far down his head the hat would sit.

Bernardo in 2006, following an extraction   Bernardo in 2007, shown with his grandfather

Throughout all the treatment we could give the boy, he remained the sweet, accepting patient about whom all pediatric dentists dream. We always asked Valeria how he was doing, and she would make sure that the grandfather would be told when we were in town. One year we did the local anesthetic injection and asked him to wait in the hall until he was numb. Apparently, our Spanish didn't carry the day and when his turn for treatment arrived, he was gone. Any child that can come in for dental care and get only an injection is a special patient! There was a gap in our annual meeting with

Bernardo, but we were rather shocked to see him in 2010 when three years had passed. He wore no hat for that visit, but his growth was clear to us.

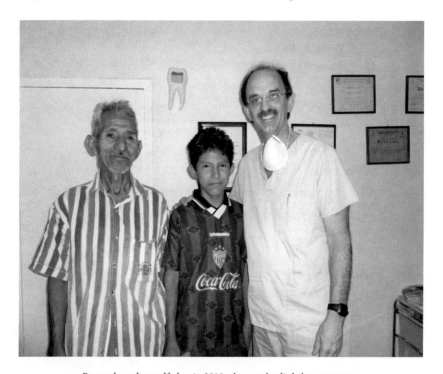

Bernardo and grandfather in 2010—he wasn't a little boy any more

My hope for being able to see more of these children was realized through the saddest of circumstances. Valeria's father, also a dentist in neighboring Ixtapa, passed away and his office, which had two chairs, enabled us to see more of the children. It also let me bring a second dentist to have the experience and help me provide more care.

Over time we saw several of the children on an annual basis and, to an extent, got to know them. Many greeted us with their smiles and enthusiasm. Few of them cried or failed to have a successful visit with us. In some cases, they wanted to show off the work we had done by opening their mouths wide so we could, ironically, admire our own work!

Look at my beautiful crowns!

Many posed for pictures with us when treatment was completed. Among my favorite memories of caring for the children was the extent to which they displayed their total comfort during their visits. I marveled at these trusting children, virtually none of whom had ever seen a dentist, yet remained receptive.

Natalie at the end of her visit

Another satisfied customer

Also unique to the project was that we worked with other Mexican professionals. There were two dentists who would come from hours-long bus rides to join us as well as local dentists who wanted to be a part of the program. Valeria's employees also participated by setting up the treatment trays and cleaning the instruments. It was an international team effort.

Some of our international team members

I have mentioned the funny or confusing moments Valeria and I have shared with our respective languages and one of the times was especially memorable. We were busy caring for the children when Valeria approached me after taking a phone call. "We are seeing the children of the garbage," she said. This was not a sentence that made any sense to me at all, but I tried to imagine what it might be. Did she really say "garage?" but that, too, brought me no closer to the reality. "What was that?" I asked. She repeated the phrase verbatim, and I simply told her I didn't understand what she meant. After some discussion among the other Mexican dentists there, she explained that we would see the children who live at the garbage dump. *Basurero* was never a word I thought would be in my limited vocabulary, but it became one that day. I had heard of situations of this sort but didn't expect to experience it in any way. She told me that she had been contacted by the director of the school there and transportation had been arranged for the children to arrive the next day.

Not knowing what to expect, I admit that I had to brace myself a bit for their entrance. When a small group of the youngsters appeared the next morning, I was pleasantly surprised to see that while their clothing was far from chic, they were not as malodorous or dirty as I might have imagined. Actually, that is exactly what I had imagined, and I was wrong. Like the patients we saw from the Octavio Paz school, these boys and girls had never been to a dentist before and yet were model patients. I occasionally wondered if their parents had laid down the law and told them not to misbehave, but from a practical standpoint, it didn't matter. They would calmly walk into the operatory, listen to our explanations of what we were about to do and then they would sit and allow us to proceed without any disruptions. They were fabulous.

Some of the children of the garbage dump

I was both stunned and curious about what life must look like for these children. The young man who had brought them to Valeria's office told us that he was so grateful for what we had done, he would be happy to do anything for us we wanted. We told him we wanted to visit the garbage dump and he said that could easily be arranged. The next day, we went. It was sometimes the condition of the teeth that broke my heart and other times it was something far beyond the mouths of the children. Somehow these hardy souls manage to survive in their environment. Unimaginable to me but normal for them, I was moved and impressed.

Left: Many "houses" were lean-to's set amidst the piles of rubbish
Right: The "main street" of the dump with houses made of available materials

Much of what I learned and appreciated by working in Zihuatanejo was that many of the boys and girls, who have far less in their lives than my patients back in Olympia, possess a durability that is admirable. It is also most likely necessary. I know that each child is a complex mix of factors, much as I was. I always appreciated the diversity of the many children I saw during my career. The Zihua children, while not perfect every time, set a high standard as dental patients. More than once the thought crossed my mind "if only ALL my patients could be like this."

CHAPTER 2

She wasn't asking for a beer

Since the project in Zihuatanejo was a one-week effort in Dra. Valeria's office, which had a single dental chair, the team that went with me was made up of three people—Diana, the hygienist, an assistant, and me. I learned quickly that Dra. Valeria worked in a very different manner than I did in the USA. The term "solo practitioner" at home meant a doctor who was the sole owner of a practice. At Dr. Valeria's office, it was more of an indication of how she worked. There were two dental assistants there, but they did not work chairside. They sat at the front desk, and they cleaned instruments, but they were not directly involved in the treatment being rendered. It was also an education of sorts for other local dentists who would come to observe the way we were practicing. Not only were they interested in the actual procedures being done, but they indicated surprise at having an extra pair of hands helping as the appointments proceeded. This is changing at many offices in Mexico, but during our first few years in Zihua, our volunteer assistants were the only ones who would literally have a hand in the care.

It was not difficult to get dental assistants to join us for these trips. Good-hearted people are everywhere and the reasons for going were as diverse as the women who went. Some had a tremendous need and desire to help children. Some wanted the opportunity to travel and experience a different culture. Living in Olympia, Washington, some simply wanted to get away from the cloudy days of November and have a chance to get more Vitamin D on the lovely beaches of the area. One year the woman who had volunteered to be our assistant had a family emergency at the last moment and contacted me to say that she just couldn't go on the trip. It was disappointing, since she had been on previous trips, was a wonderful assistant, and was well-liked by everyone. However, family comes first, and I told her not to worry about it, and that we would be all right.

My wife Mary Ellen, who is a nutritionist and writer, happened to be coming along on that particular trip, but her role was primarily to soak up some sun and provide company for me. When I told her that the assistant had canceled, she asked me if she could do the work. I thought about it and told her yes, that it was possible. When she asked me exactly what that would entail, I explained that her biggest tasks would be rinsing the teeth off and suctioning the saliva and water out of the children's mouths. Mary Ellen indicated that it didn't seem all that hard and was willing to help out. We'd been married for several years, but, until that trip, the entirety of her dental experiences had been sitting in the chair as a patient. A quick learner, she understood the procedures she would be asked to do and made headway on the technical skills required. I was sprayed more than once when the air-water syringe blasted into a child's mouth before the suction was up and running, but it was better for me than "soloing," since that would slow the treatment down considerably. I appreciated her willingness. I can now report that years later, Mary Ellen has become an adept dental assistant, not only with the technical aspects, but also with the understanding of what was being done, which instruments were needed and how to mix the various materials that went into children's mouths. During her first stint in Zihua, though, she also experienced part of the magic of pediatric dentistry that I had always mentioned to her. To hear a story is one thing, but to experience it is quite another.

Early in my volunteering days in Mexico, my Spanish was somewhere between poor and pitiful. I had purchased three entire sets of CDs to learn by listening and repeating and I was steadfast in my commitment. I had downloaded the CDs onto my iPod and attached it to my noise-reduction headphones while I mowed our yard. Living on 9.4 acres, the Springtime mowing would require about six hours or more since the grass was both long and wet. I bounced along on my rider mower repeating the phrases that came into my ears and I refused to move on to the next lesson until I could flawlessly make it through the current one. Progress was steady, but the distance I had to go to obtain anything resembling conversational skills was great. The CDs did not include any dental terminology, but fortunately one of the dental assistants in my Olympia office was fluent in Spanish, so I could ask her for the Spanish equivalents to the child-friendly terminology that I used. It was certainly helpful, and I quickly reached a level of comfort with guiding children through dental appointments in their native tongue. They seemed to follow me. The problem arose when they said something back to me. Apparently, they had not learned their Spanish from the same CDs I had. Many of the words that flew into my ears were not familiar to me. That, plus the pace of their speech far exceeded any speed limits I had mastered, and the result was a mostly one-way conversation. Undaunted, I kept chipping away in hopes of realizing my dream of becoming as comfortable and conversant in Spanish as I had become in German. The first year my wife assisted, I had not come close.

Since we saw only a limited number of patients, it wasn't difficult to recall some of them. If nothing else, I could recognize the fillings or crowns in their mouths as treatment I had completed the previous year or so. However, there were some children whose behavior I could also remember. Some were good and some were not so good. Some were simply awful. On one occasion, with my still somewhat-limited-skilled wife by my side, Valeria ushered the next child into the office, and it took only a moment to recall her utter resistance to our treatment attempts the year prior. Beatriz was not a happy camper when she entered our space the last time, and she not only screamed, but she also was physically resistant by thrashing on the chair when we tried to calm her down. Pediatric dentists learn that verbal resistance is one of the coping tools children have in difficult situations, and it rarely keeps us from moving ahead with care. Crying is actually normal. Frankly, it's one of the reasons I like working with children. I don't have to guess what they are thinking or feeling. They just let it out. Physical resistance, however, is a different matter. When we have our high-speed equipment in their mouths, if children suddenly move or thrash, the hand piece has no sense of its own. It can cut through tooth enamel, the hardest structure in the human body, so it takes little imagination to guess what it can do to tongues, lips or cheeks. It is for this reason that a child who is unable to hold still is not a good candidate for dental treatment. One look at Beatriz and I told Valeria that she had been too resistant the year before and I didn't think it would be wise to treat her. Valeria told me that her mother had expressed great concern because Beatriz had a toothache and was now ready to have it fixed. Skeptical, I relented. I put my concerns aside, greeted the girl with my best smile and invited her to take a seat. She did. I asked her how she was, and she spoke. I wondered if it was simply Señorita Hyde that had shown up the year before and now Señorita Jeckel was in my chair. As I always do, I spoke with Beatriz before diving into her mouth. I wanted her to know that I recognized her as a person, not simply another mouth. I was pleasantly surprised to see and hear her with such a calm and engaging demeanor. So far, so good. When it came time for the work to begin, I swabbed the topical anesthetic on her cheek, and she continued to sit quietly. The injection went well and likewise the place-ment of the rubber dam. Ready to move on, I could see that her lower left first primary molar had a cavernous cavity, and I knew it would require a primary tooth nerve treatment (pulpotomy) and a stainless steel crown. To her great credit, Beatriz never moved, never cried, and never resisted. She continued to look into my eyes the entire time, and I did my best to provide a play-by-play of what was happening. When treatment was complete, we removed the rubber dam, and I took her out to her mother to tell her what an excellent patient Beatriz had been. As with all mothers, Beatriz's mom was very grateful and thanked me profusely. I told her it was my pleasure. When I returned to the chair, my wife sensed that something special had happened. It had. This would be cause for celebration that night and would become a part of my lore. I didn't know it was only Act One.

The following day, echoing the words I'd heard on the mobile dental bus in California, Valeria stepped into the operatory and told me that I had a special patient who wanted to see me. Secretly I hoped it might be Luz in spite of the thirty years that had passed since that seminal moment in my life. It wasn't. It was Beatriz. She confidently strode in with a huge smile on her face and I asked her "Que tal?" meaning, what's happening? She said to me, "Quiero otra corona." I have already explained my flawed and minimal skill at understanding the children when they talk to me in their vernacular at warp speeds. In this case, I completely understood what Beatriz had said to me. The phrase, "quiero otra corona" is one that I have actually used on occasion, but more often in a restaurant. The word corona, in Spanish, means "crown." It's also the name of a popular Mexican beer. I was pretty sure I understood which one she wanted. Now a fully confident and proud patient, Beatriz didn't even wait for an invitation. She jumped into the chair, opened her mouth, and all but stated, "let's get going." I wasn't sure of her dental training, but her diagnosis was correct. On the other side of her mouth was the twin monster cavity in the equivalent tooth and I instantly knew that we were headed for another stainless steel crown. She already knew the steps as she gently nodded her head to each explanation I gave, and this time we could work through the appointment with ease and facility. The child who had been unmanageable a year earlier had become a model patient. My wife got the message. Her smile was as big as Beatriz's as we took this photograph at the end of her second appointment.

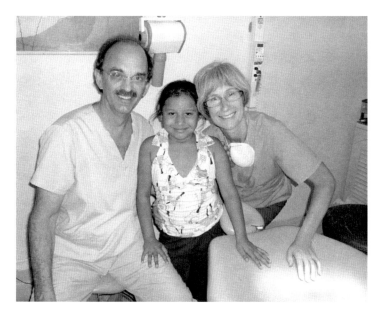

Beatriz at the end of her "otra corona" visit

My wife was thrilled to witness both the technical and the emotional sides of pediatric dentistry during that day. She said, "It's amazing to see a tooth that starts out with a big, black hole in it, and then, a few minutes later, it either has a shiny crown on it or it looks just like a regular tooth again." That is satisfying, but for me seeing the looks on the faces of the children and the parents is the reward I enjoy the most. Those crowns I placed in Beatriz's mouth are long gone, but the memory of the experience stays with me.

That evening during dinner as I enjoyed my enchiladas, refritos and chips. I also basked in the moments we had experienced together and the knowledge that Mary Ellen had gotten a taste of what makes my specialty so special. When the waiter came by to ask, "Algo mas?" (anything else?) I just couldn't resist. I told him, "Quiero otra Corona."

CHAPTER 3

The Godfather

The patients we treated in Zihua were primarily from the Octavio Paz elementary school. The principal was extremely helpful in arranging times so Valeria could examine the children and determine who would be good candidates for the clinic. I was amazed by the way so many of these children trusted us and allowed us to work in their mouths with very little resistance. When Valeria asked if I wanted to see the school itself, I immediately said I did. Located high up on a steep hill and overlooking Zihuatanejo Bay, the view property would easily have brought millions of dollars if it had been situated in an American city. However, it was not. It was the location of a school so basic that I was somewhat shocked to see it. It appeared to be constructed of pallets, planks, chicken wire for windows and sheets of corrugated steel for roofing. The floors were dirt, but the children were dressed in clothing that was clean and pressed. It was hard to imagine that a school could look like this, but my experiences were limited to my American life.

The school building in 2006

Inside the classroom

As the school construction was improving, we would enjoy going to look at the progress. We appreciated the way the buildings that had been so very basic were becoming increasingly modern and, I felt, a healthier learning environment. Parts of the school, such as the kitchen and the cafeteria, remained quite simple, but the classrooms looked more and more like a school I might have attended. We were thrilled to know that things were looking up for the children and each visit seemed to provide us with greater hope for their future.

In 2013 Valeria did not just *ask* me if I wanted to go to the school, but essentially *told* me that "we are going to the school." The drive up the steep hill never became routine for me as I listened to the car engine straining to pull our car full of people up to the peak. The rocky and mildly steep entry way into the school itself always posed a challenge to my sandaled feet, but the effort was always worth it to see new buildings going up and the site looking better each time. The principal guided us on a tour of the construction underway and, after the tour was over, asked me to join him in the cafeteria, which was a concrete slab with a ramada roof. When we arrived, many children were gathered under the ramada and with the help of Valeria, I understood that they wanted to sing us a song, both in Spanish as well as their own native dialect. Many of the students lived in the outlying hills and did not grow up with Spanish as their first language. It was fascinating that in Mexico, Spanish would be a topic of instruction. Of course, in the United States, we teach English, so it probably shouldn't have been a surprise.

The children awaiting my arrival under the ramada

Following the singing and the recitation of a poem, the principal began speaking to me. As was often the case, I could follow parts of his conversation, but other parts were left to my imagination. Valeria asked me if I had understood what he had said. "No," I had to admit. Her translation was surprising and heart-warming. She told me that the students of the sixth-grade class were requesting that I be the "padrino" for their graduation ceremony. Padrino was not among my limited vocabulary words, so before accepting, I asked what it meant. Valeria told me that padrino can mean either godfather or sponsor. Wanting assurances that I was not about to sign up for becoming the godfather for 40 children, I said that it was an honor, as long as the title reflected only the sponsorship. Once agreed, I was invited to join the children, many of whom had been patients over the years.

This picture says more than words I could write to describe the moment

The following July Mary Ellen and I were the guests of honor at the graduation. We were seated center stage at the head table on a basketball court where the ceremony would take place. As we sat quietly in our chairs, sweat ran down our backs from the summer heat. Being from Washington State, we just weren't accustomed to the degree of heat pouring down on us. The ceremony was marked by a band playing, the children marching, and proud parents gathered around the periphery. The children were all dressed in white shirts and blue pants or skirts. It was a dignified and wonderful time, even though we were broiling. I got to make a short speech and we then took the entire class to a breakfast in downtown Zihuatanejo. I have never had breakfast with 40 children and several teachers, but this one felt as natural as can be expected when in a foreign country. My years of working on the project and getting to know the people made it feel as though it was *not* a foreign country as I watched these sweet, enthusiastic children sitting together over their eggs and fruit.

The table of honor   My short moment on the mike

Breakfast for the children   The whole class—we are under the bell tower

In my own way, I am as pleased as I'm sure the families are that the school has now largely been completed. It a joy to see, considering how it was when I first saw it. We were again honored by the students in 2019 when we were in Zihuatanejo to treat the children. The entire student body assembled and with significant pomp and circumstance, played music, marched, and again made us feel very special. When people tell me how wonderful it is that I do this work, I can only smile, knowing that it would not be possible for them to understand what I receive from doing it. The trust of the children is already enough, but to have an entire school express its own gratitude is worth more to me than money. After all, here I am still writing about events of 2013-4, meaning that those memories and those moments go on long after any potential income would have been spent.

The opportunity to be a padrino for the graduating class of Octavio Paz school was an honor that I could not imagine. Watching the school go from its humble beginnings to a modern, lovely facility is likewise a source of satisfaction for me even though I have no children of my own in the school. I hold these things in my heart and maybe if I lowered my voice into the gravelly bass category and became more sullen, I might feel more like a godfather. For now, I am content carrying the title of sponsor. Godfather can wait.

The band (right) playing with the director in the lead

CHAPTER 4

I never asked for this

I have always had a fascination with the presidents of the United States and, until recently, held them in very high regard. When I was a young boy living in Elmhurst, I had a poster on my bedroom wall that had all the presidents with a picture and brief description of them. It provided the first clue that I possessed an excellent memory. By the time I was in kindergarten, I could name all the presidents in order. I still can. My father loved to show off my knowledge when we got together with family or friends. He would ask me (for example), "Who was the fourteenth president?" I would dutifully respond, "Franklin Pierce." Everyone would stare in awe and, at times, even applaud. I didn't ask for that, but I got it anyway. The greatest part about it, although I didn't appreciate it at the time, was that few people knew who *any* of the presidents were, in order, other than George Washington. It was a can't-lose proposition. In reality, I *was* correct all of the time. On the less impressive side, there had been only thirty-four presidents when I was five years old. Now, in 2022, we have had forty-six, so it would be considerably harder for a kindergartner to learn them. When my wife suggested recently that learning something new is good for an aging brain, I decided to memorize the vice-presidents. It took me about a week or so, but I learned them all, and could rattle them off to my wife. I could not, however, answer a question like, "Who was the twenty-sixth vice-president?" Also, I did not retain these names. Maybe I needed the awe and applause after all.

The volunteers were busy with patients at Dra. Valeria's office in Ixtapa when the phone rang, and Valeria spent a few minutes in conversation. Of course, I couldn't follow what was being discussed, but I thought it was probably an emergency patient, so I continued to care for the patient in the chair without interruption. As I was nearing the end of the appointment for the child, Valeria came to me and said, "The president is coming here tomorrow to visit." There are numerous moments in my communications with her that fly over my head, but they are more usually in Spanish. We do have our English moments, too. This was one of them. Thinking that perhaps I had been distracted by the care I was finishing, I asked Valeria what she had said, and she repeated in very clear and unhesitating English, "The president is coming here tomorrow to visit." Before crafting my next sentence, I thought for a moment, and considered several possible presidents who might be visiting. It might be the president of the local dental society, the president of a service club, like the Lions Club, or it might be the president of a bank, a homeowners' association, or a local dental supply company. I certainly didn't think it would be the president of Mexico. I didn't even know his name and certainly couldn't name all his predecessors in order. While each of my guesses had potential, I was curious why they would visit. Stumped, I finally posed the obvious question. "Which president?" I asked. Valeria's answer at once confused and amused me. "The president of Zihuatanejo," she said. Still another item to add to my understanding of Mexico, I discovered that in Mexican cities, the word "mayor" is spelled p-r-e-s-i-d-e-n-t.

I am grateful for politicians. I am also grateful for fire fighters, police, garbage collectors, and many other positions that I would never want. Today's world has taken politicians off a pedestal and put them in the cross hairs of media commentators and writers. I don't envy them. I enjoy my anonymity and appreciate that my fulfillment is self-generated without requiring any votes. I also have tremendous gratitude for *not* being made into a cartoon character, the butt of comedians' routines, or the focused attention of a secret service detail following me everywhere. I am continually amazed that people want these jobs.

The next day I wondered if there would be an entourage of dignitaries, media, and bodyguards when the president arrived. Other than a single newspaper reporter and a photographer, the entourage was only two people. Sadly disappointing, the president, himself, did not appear, but his wife and her public relations assistant did. Lucia was tall, impeccably dressed, poised, and spoke some English. She appeared to be the perfect first-lady of Zihuatanejo. Her interest in the project was due to her husband's recent election. Also, she wanted to assist in any way she could to support the work we had been doing for the children of their city. The project had been ongoing for twelve years at this point, but I was happy to know that the possibility existed for some help. The conversation was pleasant, sincere, and heartfelt. My sense was that her interest was not just political. Once the conversations were completed, she told me that everyone involved in the project would be invited to their home for a dinner to honor us for our work. It was quite a surprise and of course, we accepted immediately. It's not every day that one gets a presidential invitation.

The other volunteer with us on that trip was a dear pediatric dentist friend from London, Ontario. Clyde was like a brother to me. His manner, his philosophy of treating children, and his sense of humor all aligned uncannily with my own. My wife mentioned that talking to Clyde was very much like talking to me. He is an internationally known expert on care for children with special needs. I treasured the opportunity to watch and learn from him as he masterfully managed children with whom he did not have a common language. Actually, he did have a common language, but it wasn't the spoken sort. He weaved his magic, and, within minutes had a frightened, crying child sitting in his lap or lying on the chair, happily getting the teeth checked. I admired his skill. As I have always said, the health care professions are referred to as "practices." I long ago decided that when I felt I knew everything about dentistry, I would retire. Watching Clyde work provided me with the chance to see how effective his gentle approach worked. When I indulge myself in the thought that I am "really good with children," I am redirected to the realization that there is always room for improvement, as witnessed by Clyde's' skill set. When we told Clyde that we'd been invited for dinner at the president's house he, much like everyone else, expressed surprise and joy.

The night arrived and we were driven up one of the many lush, green hills in the area. When we pulled up to a walled home, we were escorted into the backyard patio area where the view of the ocean was breathtaking, and the hospitality of the hosts was wonderful. We met the president, and I had the chance to practice my Spanish with him. At times I fear that my far-from-perfect skill with the language might result in thoughts that a caveman had come back to life to dive into the mouths of local children. However, both he and his wife were very accommodating in every way, and my concerns quickly disappeared. In fact, nobody present was speaking both languages perfectly, so I stopped worrying about my Spanish.

Mary Ellen and me with the president and his wife

The meal was served on a very long banquet table. The many participants gathered around the table and toasts were made, meals were served, and some speeches ensued. Having traveled internationally on many occasions, I have become accustomed to hearing words that do not register in my limited knowledge, and this was one of those times. There were only three non-Mexicans at the gala, so Spanish carried the evening. I could tell from all the smiles, the shakes of heads, and the applause, that the entire event was positive and celebratory. Even without understanding the words themselves, I understood the feelings and the sense of what was said. I can only imagine it must be the same for the patients we see in Zihuatanejo—they didn't always understand what was happening, but they understood the feelings and the sense of what we were doing.

The evening was warm in every sense of the word. Zihuatanejo in November is typically short-sleeve weather, and the comradery that was shared only added to the glow in my mind and my heart. While he was not among the thirty-four names I had memorized as a five-year-old boy, I took a moment to savor the thought that I was dining with the president. I never asked for this, but unlike the names of the vice-presidents, I won't forget it.

CHAPTER 5

Getting a toehold in Cabo San Lucas

Once I had successfully convinced Gayle to give me the opportunity to help the children of Cabo San Lucas, she convinced her own dentist to let us use his private office for two mornings. Other than Valeria's office in Zihuatanejo, I had not been in a dental office in Mexico, so I was both intrigued and concerned about the prospects. Along with Diana, my hygienist, we selected the assistant who we wanted most to accompany us. Her name was Tory and she had been in my practice in Olympia for several years. Her quiet, calm, manner always had a positive effect on the children in my office. I was confident that she would bring that energy and caring to the children in Mexico. I wanted this initial foray to be a success, so I made sure my team was the best I could assemble.

Dr. Ramiro's office was in a part of town that I had never visited. Fortunately, Gayle came to our hotel and led us to his office, where we were greeted by both Dr. Ramiro and his new associate, Dr. Gilberto. It was there that I discovered that the convention in Mexico is to call dentists by their first names, so that I would become Dr. Greg. I never particularly cared for this because I never call anyone Mr. Bob or Mrs. Janice, but that was how it worked in Mexico. Dr. Ramiro had two dental chairs in his office and, while more than adequate to our needs, it was slightly old fashioned compared with what I had at home. Cuspidors, the little porcelain bowls with water swirling around, sat next to each chair so that patients could spit out the debris from their mouths. I immediately knew this would be a problem since I always used a rubber dam, thus making it impossible for children to spit. There was also no high-speed suction system. What Dr. Ramiro did have was a saliva ejector, which was popular in the United States until the faster, high speed suction devices were introduced into the dental field. Having had this same experience in Zihua, I didn't feel hindered and, as we set our instruments up, Dr. Gilberto, who was young, showed particular interest in everything we were doing.

 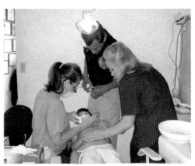

Diana and Tory *after* the patient's injection   Dr. Gilberto, watching every step we took

We had invited both doctors to observe as much as they wanted, but other than our brief introduction to Dr. Ramiro, we didn't see him very much. Dr. Gilberto, on the other hand, was literally looking over our shoulders as we began to treat the children.

The first patient was a young boy who, following the injection of local anesthetic, waved at me and flashed a huge smile as we waited for the xylocaine to take effect. Our third patient of the day was a boy who was blind, and it was then that we discovered from Gayle that no dentists in Baja California would see children with special needs. No problem, we reported. The boy's father, understandably concerned, stayed in the room as we began treatment for his son. As all proceeded along a favorable pathway, he eventually left, knowing that his child was in good hands. It was a good, reinforcing, wordless statement of support for us.

Caring for our patient who was blind

After two or three more patients, Gayle came to us and said that she was having a hard time believing what she was seeing. "This is what we do," I explained. I felt like Luz in the mobile clinic, peeling the doubt away from Gayle's eyes, much as Luz had done for me.

Now convinced that what we said was what we could do, Gayle found a remote facility where we could come one week per year to care for the children of single parents. Niños del Kapitan is a facility built by donations and includes children between the ages of two and eight. Regular classes, from kindergarten to third grade were held there. A nursery, a day-care, and a pre-school were also a part of the facility. When built, the compound included an office for a physician and one for a dentist. Since there no dentist was there when we came to town, the clinic was made available to us. I would often chuckle when people would ooh and aah when I told them I had a volunteer clinic in Cabo San Lucas. I'm sure the mental image they would conjure hardly matched the reality of the location of this place. We drove out of town onto dirt roads that were rutted and dusty until we arrived at an apparent oasis in the neighborhood. The children were all in different colored aprons, depending on which class they attended, so we quickly learned that second graders were in gray, the third graders were in green and so forth. Perhaps the best part of this phase of the Cabo project was that the children were all on-site, so that we never exhausted our supply of patients. We simply had to request two more patients and the director would have them in the waiting room within moments. There were things we didn't have, such as x-rays, but we always made the most of what was there. Upon our arrival, there would be a bench filled with children and their parents and by the end of the day, we would occasionally assemble some of our patients for a photograph.

The start of our day with patients awaiting their turns

The end of our day with the children we had seen

During the years at El Kapitan, we would be a team of three people—a hygienist, an assistant and me. There were variations in the makeup of the team, but we never needed more people since the space was small and there was only a single chair available. We did, on occasion, encounter some difficulties. The compressor was feisty, not always firing up when the switch was thrown and one year, when trying to lower the dental chair, it refused to stop as it relentlessly descended to the floor. Not satisfied with frustrating us in our ineffective efforts to halt its movement, the chair hit the floor, and only stopped when shattered pieces of plastic came flying off the base of the chair. Once it could go no farther, it stopped and would not start again. Stuck in a particularly awkward position, we were relegated to cleaning children's teeth with a toothbrush all day. We also prayed that a technician could come to repair it. That worked out and we worked in our normal fashion the next day. It was always an adventure, including getting to the facility. Any problems we had with waking up to start the day were solved during our body-rattling ride on the roads into the clinic.

One of the roads to the clinic—not the Cabo most people had seen

In spite of the bumps and occasional nonfunctional dental equipment, we typically saw about forty children each time we went. It was a quandary for us in that we had to decide which of the compromises was most accept-able—see forty children and do a single corner of their mouths, leaving three untreated; see twenty children and do one side of their mouths so that they at least had half of a healthy mouth; or see ten children and treat them entirely. The last option was not tenable, as we knew young children wouldn't easily tolerate daily appointments. We also recognized that no matter how much time we spent there, we were not going to eradicate dental decay in this group of children. As a result, we only would see a few of the children more than once during our one-week stays. Mostly, we felt good about introducing dentistry in a positive manner to a greater number of children even though we were aware of the untreated care that we left behind.

After a few years of the program running in this fashion, I asked Gayle if it would be possible to come down more than one week per year to expand the treatment we could provide. At least one, and occasionally two of the employees of the Amigos de los Niños would be on site to translate, answer the parents' questions and help us in any way they could. This meant that the home office was not being covered when we came to town. Largely due to this, and possibly other reasons that I never learned, the answer was no. The amount of treatment that was needed and the amount we could handle were so far apart that I sometimes wondered if the project was even a good idea.

On the bright side, we enjoyed ourselves immensely and we met children that no other dentist in Baja California would see, among them Magdalena, the girl I discussed in the introduction of the book. It was also at El Kapitan that we had the delightful experience of suggesting to Elena (Section 1, Chapter 2) that she looked like a dentist which led to the heart-warming sequence of events already described. Connecting with these two children and many others went a long way to make the Cabo project special.

I have suggested that the Zihuatanejo project has been more personal because of our contact with Valeria, her family, and numerous other citizens of that city. I would be remiss if I didn't say here that the initial Cabo project at El Kapitan was also very personal for us. These children, perhaps because of their home lives, would readily run up to us, jump into our arms and give us smiles, hugs, and a satisfaction that only comes through human interactions. Even while they sat in the waiting room, they welcomed our company.

Three patients in the waiting room with Dr. Cleveland and me

In 2014, knowing that Gayle was happy with our work, but not happy with her office understaffed, I became concerned when she informed me that at the end of the week, she needed to talk to me. It felt ominous and I couldn't help thinking that our work had created too much of a nuisance for the non-profit. I expected the worst. For whatever reason, in spite of all the good fortune I had experienced in my life, I still found myself steeped in negative thoughts as I steeled myself for my discussion with Gayle.

Life has taught me that there are many surprises awaiting me and this was a major one. It was not only one of the biggest surprises of my life, but one that would prove to be challenging in many ways but rewarding beyond my expectations. When Gayle began talking to me, I was practically stunned into silence with what she had to tell me.

CHAPTER 6

I don't see how that's going to work

"We're going to build a clinic for you," Gayle started. Not sure I had understood her, I asked her to repeat what she had just said. "We received two very substantial and unexpected donations recently," Gayle said, "and when the board of directors convened, it was decided that we would build you a dental clinic so you can expand your work." I can imagine that people who win the Lottery must have a similar feeling—disbelief. As my mind tried to process what I had just heard, Gayle smiled at me. "The board members who have visited you were so impressed with your work," she continued, "that they felt the best use of the funds would be to help you treat more children." I wanted details.

The ADLN office is located in a neighborhood that is filled with identical houses. They are modest and single story. I had been in the building several times over the years of the project and was familiar with the floor plan. It had three rooms, none of which were big enough for a dental clinic. Also, I wondered where the staff would work if the clinic took over the space. As it turned out, the plan was grander than I might have dreamed. Space was being made available by removing the roof and adding a second floor. The new arrangement would include a room for the audiology project, a room for the eye doctors to do their examinations, and the dental clinic. My space would be two to three times the size of the other rooms. An architect had drawn preliminary plans, and I immediately recognized a possibility that had not been considered. If one of the two upstairs bathrooms could be eliminated, the clinic space could be expanded enough to allow three chairs to fit into it. With three chairs, we could automatically triple our care. I was thrilled.

The following year the construction was underway. The roof was gone, and a large concrete pumping truck poured the walls of the upper floor. I got my first look at my future dental home.

It was exciting, but also dripping wet, with 2x4's holding up concrete forms. There were a couple of windows where I really didn't want them. Luckily, that could be changed, and new ones were Inserted at my request. One year after that, the structure was completed, and Diana joined me in designing the cabinetry and figuring out how to equip the new facility. I had learned in 1981 how difficult it was to open a new office when I lived in the city. Trying to coordinate the construction of the space in Cabo San Lucas when I was living in Olympia, Washington, posed a new challenge. It was frustrating at times, but progress was steady. The clinic opened in May, 2016, with a Team that included Dra. Valeria and Dra. Maria. Both of them told me that since I had come to Zihuatanejo to help the children there, they wanted to help the children of Cabo San Lucas and be in support of my new clinic. Now working in a virtual miniature duplicate of my office in Olympia, treatment went well and, considering it was the first session, almost without serious problems.

The results of working with Dr. Psaltis, as per my wife

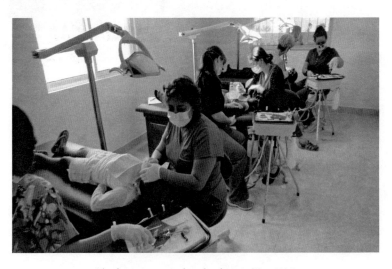

The first team to work at the clinic in May, 2016

As we eventually worked out all the various challenges, it wasn't long before we were seeing 130-140 children per session. Better yet, I was recruiting five Teams per year, meaning that the project was now providing comprehensive care for 600 or more children per year, which was a fifteen-fold increase over El Kapitan.

My first recruitment was at the national meeting of the American Academy of Pediatric Dentistry in Seattle, Washington. During my lecture, I casually mentioned that I was launching a volunteer clinic in Cabo San Lucas. I had brought two sheets of paper for those interested to sign up. When half the audience came forward during a break, I quickly found four more pieces of paper. More than 150 people signed up. The word spread and others began to recruit friends and fellow professionals. Both productivity and enjoyment increased. When told how wonderful it is that I do this, I always respond by saying, "Yes, it is wonderful for *me* that I do this." All volunteers understand this. The adage about it being better to give than receive is manifested each time I go on the project. To date, I have been with every group. My wife and I set up the clinic, guide the volunteers to our favorite restaurants as much as they want, and oversee the operation. I am fortunate to receive many contributions from dental supply companies, in part because I am a known speaker, but mostly because these companies are very generous with their support of humanitarian work.

I haven't done all of this on my own. To date I have had just under one hundred different volunteers representing thirteen states in the USA, two provinces in Canada and four Mexican states. I track the productivity of the work we provide and in May of 2021, just over five years after opening the clinic, the value of the treatment that we had provided for the children surpassed $1,000,000. More important to me, however, is the satisfaction we've all received from seeing the children succeed in our setting.

This book began with the story of Magdalena. In the introduction, I wrote that she has now been a patient in the new clinic for the past six or seven years, and each time she comes in, she still displays that winning smile, arms raised, wordless noise, and hugs for all. For us her story remains "muy especiál," no less than it did on the day of her first successful visit with us.

My receptive Magdalena along with Mary Ellen and me

Other children have been equally receptive and have given us the pleasure of helping them as well. I cannot recall each name, but I would hope that the pictures of their faces, all taken at the *end* of their appointments, tell the story better than my words.

In 2019 I was approached by a man who is constructing an enormous building in San Jose del Cabo, a city that is about 25 miles away from Cabo San Lucas. His vision is to create a community center that will include boys' and girls' clubs, a food bank, and classes for local adults to become qualified to have jobs beyond gardener or maid. Knowing about the Amigos de los Niños dental clinic in Cabo San Lucas, he asked if the non-profit could create a clinic in his new building. At some point, I will stop thinking that things can't get better. Once the building has been completed and equipped, it will have four dental chairs and the possibility exists that even more children can be seen annually.

The focus of the Cabo clinic is not the numbers of children seen or the dollars generated. It is, in many ways, a means of crossing cultural divides and making a difference for children who would otherwise have no chance of receiving dental care. In addition to the children with special needs, we routinely see children who live in foster care. They have been taken from their own homes since the environments in them were deemed unsafe. I believe we provide a sense of stability for them, since we see these children regularly. I also believe we demonstrate in our actions that people are good enough to take the time, energy, and expense to come voluntarily and help others.

Support has come from many people in many ways, and, without it all, this project would not exist. My hope is that the project will go on when I am no longer a part of it. I believe it might be my enduring legacy. If I had been asked about all of this as a possibility, I'm sure I would have replied, "I don't see how that's going to work." I no longer make statements like that. If one remains open to new possibilities and accept the many gifts that are everywhere present, I believe anything is possible.

"I've heard tell that what you imagine sometimes comes true."
- Roald Dahl

CONCLUSION

Fortunately, the conclusion of this book is not the conclusion of my career. Perhaps by fate, or perhaps by a step-by-step progression, I found my way back to treating Latino children to enable my passion to continue. This would have been hard to imagine when I fell in love with the specialty in California's Central Valley. Many people have influenced my career, and, without each of them, I would not be writing this book.

I miss my private practice. My office was a place of communion. This is not in the religious sense, but rather a time when people came together for a common goal and, in the process, created stories that will live with me until the end of my life. It was my university of life and a source of pleasure and satisfaction that I sense not all people obtain in their work. Much of my career was based on my attitude, but without those rare, life-changing moments, it may never have occurred. My evolution from a fearful patient of Dr. Wainwright to an educator and a dental missionary is a story that was propelled by those critical moments and those people who stepped up just when I needed some assistance.

My stories are in some ways unique. At the same time, similar versions could have been told by many pediatric dentists. While I have focused on my own experiences, the specialty generates stories every day for the many dentists whose practices are limited to children. I am still amazed by the growth of my specialty from the pariah it seemed to be in 1975 to arguably the most popular one as I write this. If all of my peers are enjoying their careers like I have enjoyed mine, I would hardly be surprised. If my own efforts to extol the virtues of pediatric dentistry have triggered a desire in others to pursue it, I am more than pleased that I could influence them.

The circle of life is a popular theme, and the reader will note that my own history is a good example of that. I can only hope that others can take inspiration from my words and seek out all the good there is the world—in work, in family, in giving of one's time. This is the recipe that made my life richer and more fulfilling. I am saddened by the ingress of corporate dentistry into the profession. I feel that the focus in these practices is profit. In my own career, I always felt that the *goal* was providing excellent care, and the *result* was profitability. I do not believe the converse is true. Young dentists face enormous debts from their schooling and increasing competition as more dental schools are graduating dentists into the economy. In spite of these potential downsides, I remain optimistic about the future. While children and their parents are different in some ways, the interchange between dentist and pediatric patient can remain based on that special relationship I have described. I trust that this vital factor in successful pediatric dental visits will never change in the pursuit of dollars.

For myself, my own fiscal success came as a great shock to me. Having grown up the son of a tire salesman, my childhood vacations were spent at Lake Winona in northern Indiana. A small green cabin happily housed our family of five and catching bluegills or rowing a creaky old boat was fun enough. This, too, was a life lesson to me that it didn't take a lot of money to create meaningful memories. The stories, cards, pictures, and letters depicted in this book cost me nothing, but were priceless. If this book can convey that simple observation, then I will consider my effort worthwhile. If readers have chuckled, cried, or were surprised by what they read, I will also consider my book a success. More than anything, though, my motivation was to bring a new picture of dentistry to the public. My viewpoint is not a neutral one. As I have said, "I only treat children." At 73 years of age, I credit much of my current attitude, health, and happiness with my life to that simple choice. It remains a mystery to me why people think it is strange that anyone would choose only to treat children. This book is my answer.

ACKNOWLEDGEMENTS

As with any book, many people were involved in making this one possible. Very special thanks to Phil Varney for his brilliant editing of my first draft. As a retired English teacher, he not only "came out of retirement" to do me this incredible favor, but also taught me that in spite of my own high opinion of my grasp of the English language, I still have much to learn.

To Wendell, Russ, and Anna, for their encouragement, suggestions, and criticisms of my initial draft. It was important for me to have non-professionals read this to make sure I wasn't overly technical in my dental stories.

To my parents, a special thank you for giving me the opportunity to live a life beyond my own expectations. While my commentary about my father may have seemed harsh, I recognize that it was his way of encouraging me to always be my best. My mother, who is lightly mentioned in this book, was always patient with me and supportive in all my efforts. It is undoubtedly her patience that I inherited, which led to much of the success in my career. Without the two of them, I'm certain my career and, therefore, this book, would not have been possible.

Black and white drawings by Ryan Alexander-Tanner

Painted pictures by Erica Psaltis-Medici

GLOSSARY OF PEDIATRIC DENTAL TERMINOLOGY

Decoding scientific terminology into children's language

Blow sugar bugs- clean a tooth of decay

Button- the clamp used to hold the rubber dam in place

Count teeth- exam the teeth

Magic air- nitrous oxide

Pictures of your teeth- x-rays

Put teeth to sleep- giving local anesthetic to numb the teeth

Raincoat- rubber dam

Sleepy juice- local anesthetic

Straw- suction for removing saliva and water

Sugar bugs- dental caries, or decay

Take tooth pictures- x-rays

Toothpick- explorer for checking the teeth

Tooth tickler- slow speed hand piece, also used for cleaning the teeth

Tooth vitamins- topical fluoride

Whistle- high speed hand piece

Wiggle a tooth- extract a tooth

GLOSSARY OF ACTUAL DENTAL TERMINOLOGY

Decoding scientific terms into lay language

Caries- dental decay, usually caused by bacteria resting on the teeth

Cariogenic- causing decay. Sugar is a perfect example

Cementoclasts- specialized cells that resorb (eat away) roots of primary teeth to facilitate them coming out when the permanent successor is ready to erupt

Fluoride- a naturally occurring element that physically hardens the surface of teeth, thus making them more resistant to caries

Local anesthetic- the chemical compound used to numb specific areas or regions of the mouth (see Novocain)

Novocain- the generic term for local anesthetic, which may be of three different sorts: Lidocaine, Articaine or Mepivicaine

Prepping a tooth- "drilling," removing decay and shaping the are to prepare ("prep") it for a filling

Pulpotomy- similar to a root canal, but only involving the crown portion of the primary tooth

Sealant- a preventive material that is placed in the grooves of non-decayed permanent teeth (primarily on molars) to protect them from food impaction and likely decay

Stainless steel crown- a restoration that completely covers a badly decayed primary tooth

Third molars- known by the public as "wisdom teeth," these are the rearmost molars in the human mouth and only in some instances have adequate space to erupt and be functional. Usually there is not adequate space for them and it is for this reason that removal is often recommended

Topical anesthetic- a liquid or gel that is applied directly to the soft tissues to numb the area prior to insertion of the local anesthetic needle